The Nature and Mission of the Church

The Nature and Mission of the Church

Donald G. Miller

John Knox Press
Richmond, Virginia

To
LYNNE, DOUG, and DICK
members
of
the church
in
our house

Ninth printing 1969

Standard Book Number: 8042-3208-3
Library of Congress Catalog Card Number: 57-9443

Contents

I

The Nature of the Church

The word "church" is a very flexible word. It means many things, and different things to different people. It may even mean several things to the same person. For example, one may say, "Let's go to church." To what is he going? Says another, "I grew up in the church." What does that mean? Still another may insist, "The church ought to do something about it." What is this church that he thinks should act? "We go to Dr. So-and-So's church," affirms someone else. Is it really Dr. So-and-So's church? "At my church," continues another, "we have a good youth program." In what sense can a church be *my* church? And is the church a place where programs are in order? It is often argued, "The church keeps up the moral tone of a community." Is that the business of the church? "The best people belong to the church," we are sometimes told. Is the church, then, the society of the socially and morally acceptable?

These various expressions show how vague and uncertain is our idea of the church. It is strange that we can say so many different things about the same word. It is well, therefore, to face the question of what the church really is.

Popular Conceptions of the Church

Our search for an answer to this question may well be prefaced by a look at some of the popular ideas men have of the church. To some the church is a building. On a plot of ground at the corner of a farm, or on a village square, or on the busy street of a bustling city, or nestling in a narrow ravine made by a row of skyscrapers in a modern metropolis, there stands a building—and to many, that building is the church. We can point to it, as we do the store, or the bank, or the theater, and say, "There is the church." Even one who never darkens the door of that building may be heard to say, "I pass the church every day on my way to work."

Others, aware that even a bank, or a store, or a theater is far more than a building—for a bank without financial transactions is not a bank, nor a store without goods a store, nor a theater without actors or film a theater—see that the church is not merely the building which goes by that name, but in some way exists in the people and the activities which go on in the building. To them, the church is like a club, or a lodge, or a fraternity. It is a group of like-minded people who enjoy each other's company. By their own choice they have banded together in a human organization for mutual benefit or enjoyment. They give money to keep the building in repair, to heat it in winter and to cool it in summer, and to support the various activities in which they engage. This provides a stimulus to the native religious side of their nature, and offers them a channel for social fellowship with a high type of people.

Some who are more outgoing in their desire to help other people think of the church as an effective social agency. It exists basically to serve the needs of the poor, or the unfortunate, or the uneducated. It is a society where social passion is to be kindled and maintained by religion. Its goal is humanitarianism. But since men are notoriously unlikely to be humane to others without the gracious influences of religion, the church exists to provide the religious energies which will conquer man's cruelty and quicken his kindness. The church might well be thought of as the religious arm of the community chest, or a Society for the Prevention of Cruelty to Human Beings.

Another view of the church is that it consists of an audience which comes weekly to listen to a great orator. A man gifted in speech and dynamic in personality, with perhaps a flair for the dramatic and the ability to produce emotion, gathers around him a group of followers who so love to hear him speak that they would not miss him for anything. This is what leads people to speak of "Dr. So-and-So's church." To them, that particular church is made up of this remarkable pulpiteer and the loyal group of people who enjoy hearing him speak, or who feel that they get great good from his sermons. It is this also which frequently causes congregations to dwindle and wither away a few short months after such a man leaves a community for another one.

Several other ideas of the church may be added to these. Sometimes the church is thought of as a place where people come to get their problems solved—a sort of religious clinic. Again, the church is often understood to be a society for moral culture, a type of religious gymnasium where moral and spiritual exercises are designed to maintain or increase the moral health of individuals. Or, once more, many think of the church as the historic extension of some great past event. It is a society whose purpose is to perpetuate the memory of Jesus or the beginning of the Christian group, much as the D.A.R. rekindles the memory of the American Revolution, or the Huguenot Society the beginnings of the Huguenot movement.

The plain fact with which the New Testament confronts us is that no one of these, nor all of them together, is adequate. All of them may be phases, or accompaniments, of the church's life, but none of them *is* the church. To confuse the church with them would be like saying that a fire company consists in a group of men sitting in a fire station playing cards, or that a stock exchange is a place where men huddle in groups and shout to each other amidst the endless flow of ticker tape.

What, then, is the church? We shall seek first to discover from the New Testament what the nature, or *essence*, of the church is, then to draw from this certain qualities or characteristics which necessarily follow.

The New Testament Conception of the Church

The English word "church" comes from the Greek word *kyriakon*, which means "that which belongs to the Lord." This word is used only twice in the New Testament, once to designate the Lord's Supper (1 Corinthians 11:20), and once in speaking of the Lord's day (Revelation 1:10). But "church" is especially used to translate another New Testament word which is closely related to the idea of "that which belongs to the Lord"—it is the word *ecclesia,* from which our word "ecclesiastical" comes, which describes the *"people* who belong to the Lord." This word is one of the favorite words of the New Testament, being used some 115 times. But the idea it embodies appears far more frequently than that. The New Testament writers are often speaking about "the people who belong to the Lord" when they do not use the word *ecclesia.*

The basic meaning of this word was merely a gathering of citizens summoned, or "called out," by a herald to meet in a public place, for some special purpose. It later came to be used loosely for any public assembly of people for any reason. The New Testament, however, gives to this word a very special meaning. It uses it not merely to describe *an* assembly of people, but quite consistently speaks of *the* assembly. This special use of the word has no parallel in secular Greek writings outside the New Testament. The only parallel comes from the Greek translation of the Old Testament. There the expression "the *ecclesia* of God" or "the *ecclesia* of the Lord" is frequently found. Obviously, therefore, when the New Testament writers use this expression found nowhere outside the Old Testament, they must have been using it in its Old Testament meaning. They were saying that "the church" is what the Old Testament described as those who were "called out" of the world to be "the people who belonged to God" in a very special way. This connection of the church with the Old Testament people of God is made unmistakably clear when Paul calls the church "the Israel of God." (Galatians 6:16.)

But when the church was formed, there was another Israel— the old Israel, the ancient people of God in whose veins flowed the blood of Abraham. What made the difference between this "old Israel" and the "new Israel"? The decisive thing was their attitude toward Jesus Christ. The old Israel had rejected Jesus as Messiah and had Him condemned to death. The new Israel was made up of those among the Jews who accepted Jesus as Messiah, and believed that He had been raised from the dead. They felt that the old Israel had forfeited the right to be the special "people who belonged to God" and that the Christian Church was now the true "people of God."

But they had become the "people of God" not because of anything they had done. They were such purely because of what Jesus had done. He had called them to Himself as their Messiah. They had responded to His call. They had followed Him when He was here in the flesh. They now believed that though He had been slain He was alive forevermore. They had been made "God's people" solely by the call, the life, the death, and the resurrection of Jesus. To be "the people of God," then, was identical with being "the people of Jesus." Paul could write to the Corinthian Christians that they were "the church of God" because they were "sanctified in Christ Jesus" and called "on the name of our Lord Jesus Christ." (1 Corinthians 1:2.) Again, Paul referred to the Christians at Ephesus as "the church of the Lord which he obtained with his own blood." (Acts 20:28.) Here it is plain that the Christian church was brought into being by Jesus, and that He had done it by His death—which, to Paul, always included the Resurrection as the outcome of His death. The church, therefore, is the community of those who live by the power of the death and resurrection of Jesus.

This leads naturally to the two favorite terms used in the New Testament to describe the church; namely, the *temple of the Holy Spirit* and the *body of Christ*. As we shall see, these two expressions are very closely interrelated and are practically synonymous.

The church as God's temple and as Christ's body is to be understood in the light of its relation to Jesus Christ. *He* is God's temple. The church is *His* body. Apart from Him, neither temple nor body could have any meaning for the church. Let us see, then, how this is set forth in the New Testament.

In the Old Testament, the temple—and the tabernacle before it—was the place where God had chosen to dwell in the midst of His people. It was there that God met His people and they met Him. It was there that God's glory was to be seen. It was there that God was worshiped. It was there that priests made sacrifices for sin. It was there that men came to learn God's law and to understand His will. It was there that children were dedicated to God and adults offered themselves to God as His servants. The temple was the place where every relation between a holy God and sinful man was to be established and maintained.

But the old temple had failed to achieve the ends for which it had been built. It had been desecrated and defiled, and was worthy only of being destroyed. Once, in 587 B.C., it had been destroyed. Later it was rebuilt, but the failure of the earlier temple was repeated. Instead of being the place where God met man, it had become an impediment in the way of their meeting. Jesus, therefore, in decisive and dramatic action, entered the temple in judgment, indicating that it was no longer fulfilling its purpose. Instead of being "a house of prayer" it had become "a den of robbers." (Matthew 21:13.) Jesus also had to pronounce over the temple the sad words of doom: "There will not be left here one stone upon another, that will not be thrown down." (Matthew 24:2.)

But was the purpose for which the old temple stood never to be fulfilled? Yes, it would be fulfilled. The old temple was to be replaced by another and a better one. And that temple was the body of Jesus. From henceforth, God would meet man in Him! That Jesus thus conceived of Himself is quite plain in the Gospel story. When He was on trial, one of the witnesses against Him made the charge: "This fellow said, 'I am able to destroy the temple of God, and to build it in three days.' " (Matthew 26:61.) A charge like this taken literally would have been absurd. It is obvious that it was misunderstood by the one who made it. But the charge shows that Jesus had said something about destroying a temple.

The Fourth Gospel makes plain what Jesus had meant by what He said. In John's account of the cleansing of the temple, when Jesus was asked for a sign of His authority to do it, He replied, "Destroy this temple, and in three days I will raise it up." (John 2:19.) The Jews misunderstood Him, thinking that He was talking about the temple of stone which stood before them.

But the writer adds, "he spoke of the temple of his body," and then relates the saying to the death and resurrection of Jesus. (John 2:21-22.) In this way, Jesus was claiming that the true temple of God was no longer the structure of stone which stood before them. It was rather His own body, which His enemies were planning to put to death, but which would be raised to new life on the third day. Add to this the statement in John 1:14 that "the Word became flesh and dwelt [tabernacled] among us," and it is plain that Jesus' "flesh," His "body," was the new temple of God which was to take the place of the old temple.

The old temple would be destroyed never to rise again. On the other hand, the temple of Jesus' body would be destroyed in death, but would rise again at the Resurrection. From now on, God would meet His people in Jesus. It was in Him that God's "glory" was to be seen. In Him God was to be worshiped. He was the great High Priest who made the sacrifice of Himself for man's sin. In Him men would learn God's law and understand His will. To Him children would be dedicated, and men would offer themselves to God as His servants. In Jesus, every relation between a holy God and sinful men was to be established and maintained. Hence, when He died on the cross, the curtain of the old temple was torn in two (Matthew 27:51), showing that the way into God's presence was no longer through the old sanctuary, but rather through the sanctuary of the risen body of Jesus. The true temple of God is the risen Lord!

But where does the church stand in relation to all this? Repeatedly, the church is called "God's temple" or "house." (1 Corinthians 3:16; Ephesians 2:21; 1 Timothy 3:15; Hebrews 10:21; Revelation 3:12.) It is also called "the body of Christ." (Romans 12:5; 1 Corinthians 12:27; Ephesians 1:23; 4:12; 5:30; Colossians 1:18, 24.) If the true temple of God is the body of Jesus, how can the church be God's temple? The answer to this is to be found at Pentecost. There, after Jesus had died, risen, and ascended to the right hand of God, He returned in His Spirit to live in the church. He is still the temple of God, but He is living in His church. So, by virtue of His living presence in His church, it becomes the temple of God. And that temple which was Christ's body when He was on earth is now to be found in the church, which is His body since the Resurrection. God now tabernacles among men in Jesus, as Jesus lives in His church.

The church, then, is made up of all those to whom the risen Christ has given His Spirit. It is the fellowship of those who believe in the Resurrection, and to whom the living Christ is real. Where Jesus is, there is the church. And Jesus has promised that "where two or three are gathered in my name, there am I in the midst of them." (Matthew 18:20.) The church is the new people of God, made possible by the death and resurrection of Jesus, and created by His Spirit living in their midst. That is why Peter could say of the church, "You are a chosen race, a royal priesthood, a holy nation, God's own people . . . Once you were no people but now you are God's people." (1 Peter 2:9-10.) The church is the community of the Resurrection, the fellowship of men in whom God's Spirit dwells, the fraternity of the forgiven, the people who are called out of the world to belong to God, in order that their corporate life may consist in His worship and service.

Characteristics of the Church

If this be the church, then certain characteristics follow "as the night the day." Fuller treatment of some of these must be reserved until later, but they may here be traced in bold lines.

The church is divine, not human. We do not make the church by our efforts, we receive it as a gift from God. The church is not created by a group of religious men banding together to form it. It was created by God through the resurrection of Jesus Christ. His resurrection ushered in the "new age" which shall abide when "this present age" is gone, when time shall be no more, and God shall be all and in all. This new life, "eternal life," is open to all who will receive it by faith. Those who are willing to identify themselves with Jesus Christ in His death and resurrection are already living in the sphere of His resurrection power. This no man achieves. It is the gift of God. Better organization, increased human effort, modernization of methods—all good in themselves—do not build the church. They are mere means by which the church expresses itself. Our primary task is to examine whether we are the church or not.

The church is a fellowship of faith, not an institution. The church does not consist of buildings or programs, but of people. Nor is the church made up of unbroken historic institutional forms, but of believers in the gospel. One is, therefore, not saved by outward adherence to an institution, but by faith in Christ. No one structural form of institutional life, nor any specific form of worship, is of the *essence* of the church. The church may express itself in history in many forms. Nor is the church made up of a hierarchy of clergy who dispense grace to laymen. Various functions are given to various members of the church, just as different members of the body have various functions to perform. But no one of the members, nor any group of members, *is* the church. The church is the total body of believers, clergy and laity alike, who are "in Christ" and who together make up His body here on earth. The church is not a rigid structure, but a fellowship of all those in whose corporate life the Spirit of Christ dwells.

The church is corporate, not individualistic. (The Latin *corpus*, meaning "body" or the uniting of many members into one whole, gives us the English word "corporate" which best describes the "E Pluribus Unum" which is the church.) Just as a body is not made by collecting a hand here, and an arm there, and a foot somewhere else, and then putting them together, so the church is not made up of a group of isolated individuals who decide to unite for their common religious welfare. Furthermore, just as a hand has no possible existence apart from the body of which it is a part, neither does an individual Christian have any existence apart from the total church, the body of Christ. The church is not "a bouquet of believers," a collection of individual Christians brought together by mutual agreement. The church is an organism from which each member draws his life. Christ is the church. And to be in Him is to be in the church.

Our faith is personal, but not individual. It is the personal ingrafting into a corporate reality. When a nation surrenders in war, it is not a matter of each individual making a surrender.

The corporate nation acts. The individual may go on fighting, without even knowing that the nation has surrendered. When he hears of the surrender, he must personally identify himself with the action of the corporate nation, but he cannot act as an individual. He can act only as a part of the nation. So, when Christ triumphed over evil through His death and resurrection, He won a total corporate victory for mankind. We must personally appropriate this by faith, thus making His victory our victory. But it is not an individual action. It is the personal acceptance of an act done quite outside one's individual experience, and done for the whole race. Never is one less of an individual than when he exercises personal faith in Christ. By that very act of faith, he is identified with Christ and with all others who are believers in Christ. He has moved from his corporate involvement with sin and death into a corporate involvement with redemption and life. As P. T. Forsyth has said, the "same act which sets us in Christ sets us also in the society of Christ." To be in Christ, then, is to be in His body, the church. We may neglect our relation to Christ's people, but as long as we are in Him we cannot destroy it. As the member of the surrendered nation is involved in the whole nation's action, so the believer is involved in the whole church. To join a church does not put us in the church. It merely publicly witnesses to what is already a fact.

The church is universal, not local. The church is not merely the particular congregation to which I belong, nor the denomination to which it adheres. When one unites with the church in any particular place, he unites with the church universal. The universal church is not made up by adding all local congregations together. A university is more than the sum total of the colleges which make it up. And, in one sense, the whole university is present in each of its colleges. So, rightly understood, the whole church is present in any local congregation. It is the whole people of God looking out on the world at that point. The word *ecclesia* in the New Testament is used to speak of the entire church, or of a local church, or even of a small group of Christians within a local church. The same word covers all cases. "The part is equal to the whole, because each part possesses, not a fragment of the

Christ, but the whole Christ." Where men meet in Jesus' name, there He is—not just a part of Him. The whole church is in Him, and He is in the whole church.

If it were not for the barriers of time and space, when the church meets for worship all believers, from Adam to the end of time, would be present. But although time and space make that impossible physically, it is nonetheless true spiritually. The writer of Ephesians tells us that God's purpose was "to unite all things in Christ, things in heaven and things on earth." (See Ephesians 1:10.) When any part of the church meets, then, it is in fellowship with every other part, including those already dead and those yet to be born. The writer of Hebrews tells us that we are now in fellowship with "the assembly of the first-born who are enrolled in heaven . . . and . . . the spirits of just men made perfect." (Hebrews 12:23.) To belong to the church, then, is to belong to all others who were, or now are, or ever shall be in the church. A local gathering of Christians is Christ, the whole Christ, present and making Himself known there at that point. Said Paul, "We who are many are one body." (1 Corinthians 10:17; see also Romans 12:5 and 1 Corinthians 12:12-27.) The local church, therefore, is not *a* church, it is *the* church at that place. The church is one.

The church is the body of the living Christ, not the perpetuator of His memory nor the guardian of a tradition. From what has been said above, it is plain that the church has no existence unless the Spirit of the Living Christ lives in her *now*. The church does not exist to perpetuate the "spirit" of a great man long since dead, as a Browning Society seeks to keep alive the work of the great poet. In that case it would be the body of Christ mummified, like the body of Lenin—mute witness to the life of one who was alive but is now dead, save as his memory and work are perpetuated. But the church is no mummy, no mere lingering memorial to the past. Christ lives now, and lives in the church. The church is the living vehicle of the living Lord who is very much alive now, and rules the world from His position at the right hand of God. It is only as He lives *now* in the church, that the church is the church.

As the temple of God and the body of Christ, *the church exists not for her own sake, but solely for the glory of God*. The church is a worshiping community, whose worship is designed not for what we may get out of it, but that we may return to God the love we owe. This worship is rendered to God in the outgoing of our hearts to Him in gratitude through prayer and praise. But worship consists also in service. True praise to God involves the surrender of all one is and has, to be used as an instrument in His hands for accomplishing what He wants done in the world. True worship involves "devoting the will to the purpose of God."

Consequently, the outlook of the church is not toward her self-preservation but toward the salvation of the world. As Christ had to die in order to save the world, so in her own measure the church has to die to be the instrument of that salvation. The central aim of the church, therefore, is not that of human societies, which are various forms of "co-operative egoism," or the pooling of "social self-interest." In so far as the church exists merely for the sake of serving its own members, or meeting the needs of a select few who have banded together for mutual betterment, it ceases to be the church. The church is an army, committed to the sacrifice of self, engaged in costly action in God's warfare against evil, looking forward to that day when "The kingdom of the world has become the kingdom of our Lord and of his Christ, and he shall reign for ever and ever." (Revelation 11:15.)

This look at the nature of the church is sufficient to indicate clearly that the popular conceptions of the church in the mind of many of its members are far wide of the New Testament conception. The time is overdue when the church should rethink the meaning of her own life.

2

The Life of the Church

The story of human history is the story of broken relationships. The tragedy of this, however, cannot be fully understood until it is seen in the light of what history was intended to be. The purpose of history has been sidetracked. The real story is but the shattering of a dream.

The Tragedy of Human Existence

The symphony of man's existence, as set forth in Genesis, begins in a delicate harmony. Man is made to live in fellowship with a gracious and holy God. He is set in a universe that is good. He is to utilize the rhythm and harmony of nature for constructive ends. He is to build a society wherein each person can realize his highest freedom in obedience to God, and achieve the greatest measure of self-development in the service of others. Here is the promise of harmony and beauty. Here is the echo of heaven's music on earth.

But the symphony does not proceed far before the music is marred. Discord begins to creep in. The individual instruments seem to be off key and out of tune. The rhythm of life is soon lost, with the players competing with each other in a clamor of confusion. The discord becomes louder and more intense, until the whole affair ends in chaos.

Look at the Genesis story. First, man rebels against God, so that the harmony of the fundamental relationship of life is lost.

(Genesis 3:1-10.) But when man is no longer in right relations with God, the basic securities on which human relationships rest are undermined. First, the oneness of husband and wife was broken. Eve was no longer to Adam the perfect partner in whom his own life found meaning—"This at last is bone of my bones and flesh of my flesh"!—but rather one who is over against him as a problem and a rival—"The woman whom thou gavest to be with me, she gave me fruit of the tree, and I ate." (Genesis 2:23; 3:12.) This disharmony spreads until family relationships completely break, and brother murders brother. (Genesis 4:8.) The discord overleaps the limits of the family, and touches the whole of the life of man. Commerce, culture, industry, and social relations are all marred. (Genesis 4:19-24; 6:1-4.)

The discord becomes so painful that "the Lord was sorry that he had made man on the earth, and it grieved him to his heart." (Genesis 6:6.) A fresh start with Noah after the flood gives promise of renewed harmony in history. But the promise gives way to early disappointment. Soon man is seen once more trying to rear a society absolutely independent of God, with the result that man's relation to his fellow man is again broken, and the end is Babel—disunity, confusion of tongues, chaos. (Genesis 11:1-9.) This old story from the beginnings of the race is surprisingly new. It reflects life as we know it. Our world is a sordid tangle of broken relationships. Homes are broken, friendships are marred, mutual agreements are scorned. Business is cursed by cutthroat competition, politics is a mad scramble for power at the expense of others, social snobbishness and racial pride divide men, and nations glare at each other in hatred and fear.

God's Answer to Tragedy

Is there no solution to this problem of broken relationships? Is man doomed to an endless succession of tragedy, with no promise of restoring the lost harmony of life? Does God have no answer to man's dilemma? Yes, God has an answer. The church born at Pentecost exists to bear witness that God, in His mercy in Christ, has brought harmony out of discord, has made it possible for all breaches between Himself and man, and between man and man, to be repaired. Pentecost is God's answer to Babel!

At Pentecost, the Spirit of the risen Christ was breathed into the company of believers who were gathered in the upper room. Together, they became the body of Christ, living by His Spirit within them. The new order of life into which Jesus had entered by His resurrection was now brought to earth in the fellowship of His people. The church was a new creation, a bringing into being of that which did not exist before. In this sense, it is a miracle which has no parallel in human experience. It can, therefore, never be thought of as only a sociological fact, a gathering of men which can be explained by any merely human reasons. It is rather the ingrafting of men into the resurrection body of Christ, so that the power of His risen life flows through them. Through His life which conquered death, they are already living, in some measure, in the world beyond death. The Holy Spirit, the Spirit of the risen Jesus, who belongs to the eternal world, has taken up His abode in the life of the church.

It is often asked why the Holy Spirit came at Pentecost, and not before. Was not the Holy Spirit in existence before Pentecost? And if existent, was He not at work in the world? The answer to both questions is, Yes. The Holy Spirit was very much alive and very active before Pentecost. We are told in the Gospel story that at Jesus' baptism, the Holy Spirit descended upon Him. (Mark 1:10.) Furthermore, Luke remarks that immediately after that, Jesus was "full of the Holy Spirit." (Luke 4:1.) But Jesus could not impart the Holy Spirit to His church until He had fully overcome that which separated man from God. The Fourth Gospel states that during Jesus' earthly career "the Spirit had not been given, because Jesus was not yet glorified." (John 7:39.) In other words, until Jesus died and rose again and ascended to the Father, the breach between God and man could not be overcome. But after dying our death, and then triumphing over death in the Resurrection, Jesus ascended to His Father as representative Man, taking redeemed humanity with Him. Hence, the risen Lord carried our humanity up into the God-head. Now, God and man again were one. The lost unity be-

tween them had been restored. It was, therefore, possible for
Jesus to give to men the gift of restored harmony between them
and God which He had achieved for them.

At Pentecost, that is exactly what happened. The God-man
brought the restored unity between God and man into the life
of His church. They were "all filled with the Holy Spirit." (Acts
2:4.) The life of the risen and glorified Lord flowed into the
lives of those assembled at Pentecost. In Him, they too were
again at one with God. And since they were all in Him, they
were also at one with each other. The whole tragedy of man's
broken relationships, both vertical and horizontal, was now overcome. There was a true and final reconciliation between God and
man, and between man and man. Now let us see how this expressed itself in the life of the church.

Unity

For one thing, this twofold reconciliation fused the members
of the church into a unity. The experience came not on isolated
individuals, but on the group. The Holy Spirit is the life of
Christ's body. The individual members of that body share in it
only as they are attached to the body. The whole is much more
than the sum of its parts. The life of a human body does not
consist in adding together the life of each member—a finger, an
ear, a hand, a foot—rather the finger, the ear, the hand, and the
foot derive their life from the body by being members of it. So
at Pentecost the church became a unified body from which each
member drew its life.

The Holy Spirit did not invade the lives of a few individuals
who together formed the church. The Spirit came on the whole
church to create an organism, a complete body. The effect of this
in individuals is that the life of the whole body flows through
them as members. As the life of the vital organs—heart, lungs,
kidneys—is imparted to hands, feet, eyes, so the vitality of
Christ's body is given to the various individual members of that
body. When a piece of skin is grafted on to a body, the body does
not receive life from it. On the contrary, the skin lives only as it

embeds itself in the body and becomes an actual part of the living organism, receiving its life from the body. So the church is the living organism vitalized by the Spirit of the glorified Christ. Individuals share this life by being ingrafted into Christ. The church is not made up of a group of individuals coming together, like pebbles in a bucket. That would be an aggregate, not a body; a collection of specimens, not an organism. The church is the one body of Christ Himself, into which individual members are ingrafted by faith.

This unity of the church which is something more than the sum total of the individuals who make it up, is to be seen clearly in the meaning of the words used to describe it. We are told that after Jesus had ascended, the disciples *"with one accord* devoted themselves to prayer." (Acts 1:14.) Later, "when the day of Pentecost had come, they were *all together* in one place." (Acts 2:1.) The result of the Pentecost experience was that day by day they were "attending the temple *together."* (Acts 2:46.) When persecution befell them, "they lifted their voices *together* to God." (Acts 4:24.) The whole "company of those who believed were of *one heart and soul"* (Acts 4:32), and the continuing mark of the whole Christian movement was that "they were *all together"* (Acts 5:12).

This *togetherness* meant much more than the fact that they were side by side, that they stayed constantly in close proximity to each other in one location. It was a *spiritual* togetherness expressive of a unity which went clear beyond the sum total of what each was in himself. What this togetherness was may be seen, in a bad sense, in what we know as "the mob spirit." When Stephen was stoned they "rushed together upon him." (Acts 7:57.) When Paul was mobbed at Ephesus, the people "rushed together into the theater." (Acts 19:29.) A reality is created in a mob which is quite more than the sum total of personal anger. The individual is seized by this transcendent force and carried clear beyond himself. He becomes the vehicle of evil forces which flow into him from the mob. Now it is this surpassing power which vitalizes a group and gives itself to the individuals in the group which is the secret of the unity of the church. There, in a good sense, the individual is caught up by the Spirit of Christ who lays hold of the entire group. Vital forces flow into the individual, lifting him out of himself and making him the channel of dynamic influences which could never be his alone.

The Holy Spirit is God's gift to His *church.* "They were *all* filled with the Holy Spirit . . . Peter, *standing with the eleven* . . . we *all* are witnesses. . . . great grace was upon them *all.*" (Acts 2:4, 14, 32; 4:33.) The Spirit gave Himself not to isolated individuals but to a worshiping community. To receive the Spirit was to be in the church. For individuals to have the Spirit meant that the life of the whole body was expressing itself in one of its members. St. Paul later summed up what Pentecost means in this regard: "For just as the body is one and has many members, and all the members of the body, though many, are one body, so it is with Christ. For by one Spirit we were all baptized into one body . . . and all were made to drink of one Spirit." (1 Corinthians 12:12-13.)

Proclamation

A second way by which the new life of the church expressed itself was a new understanding of what God had done for men in Jesus, and a passionate desire to be heralds of this to all men. The book of the Acts says that "they devoted themselves to the apostles' teaching." (Acts 2:42.) What was the "apostles' teaching"? It was the group understanding of the significance of Jesus as both Messiah of Israel and Saviour of the world. By coming into the life of the church through His Spirit, all that Jesus had taught when He was here on earth, and all that He had done by dying, rising, and ascending to the right hand of God, became clear.

Jesus had told the disciples before He died that when the Holy Spirit came He would teach them all things, and bring to their remembrance all that He had said to them. (John 14:26.) According to the writer of the Fourth Gospel, this is exactly what happened. In referring to the Triumphal Entry he writes: "His disciples did not understand this at first; but when Jesus was glorified, then they remembered that this had been written of him and had been done to him." (John 12:16.) The same was said of the cleansing of the temple. (John 2:22.) There were profound meanings in all that Jesus said and did which were hidden while He was on earth. He tried, for example, to teach His disciples the meaning of His death, but they failed to understand and tried to dissuade Him from going to the cross. (Matthew 16:21-23.) When Jesus finally was nailed to the cross, they all forsook Him and fled. But in the light of the Resurrection, the cross began to take on meaning for them. God had vindicated Jesus as Messiah and Lord. The path of suffering had become the path to glory.

At Pentecost, filled with the Spirit of the risen Christ, Peter set the pattern for Christ's church as a herald of the gospel. "This Jesus God raised up," he cried, "and of that we all are witnesses. . . . Let all the house of Israel . . . know assuredly that God has made him both Lord and Christ, this Jesus whom you crucified." (Acts 2:32, 36.) From then on, a characteristic mark of the church throughout the New Testament record was the heralding of the "good news" of what God had done for men in Christ. With insight, power, and courage even unto death (Stephen, for example), the fellowship of believers gave witness to their faith to all. Jesus had been God's ambassador sent from heaven to negotiate a reconciliation with His estranged enemies. As Christians who have been reconciled become the body in which He dwells, they in turn are now God's ambassadors of reconciliation to a world in rebellion against God. "Christ reconciled us to himself and gave us the ministry of reconcilation," wrote Paul. "So we are ambassadors for Christ, God making his appeal through us." (2 Corinthians 5:18, 20.)

Fellowship

Another aspect of the church's life flowing from Pentecost was a new kind of fellowship which transformed every human relationship. The life of the risen and glorified Christ which had restored the broken relationship between them and God, had also overcome every breach in the relationships between man and man. As, in the church, men were now one with God, they also were one with each other. As Paul put it: "We, though many, are one body in Christ, and individually *members one of another.*" (Romans 12:5.)

The Greek word which describes this phase of the church's life is *koinonia,* usually translated "fellowship," sometimes "communion." But the fellowship which came into being at Pentecost was not a mere deepening of ordinary human intercourse, nor the addition of one more "fellowship group" to the many others which have existed both before and after it. This fellowship was something unique. The English translation does not make clear what Acts 2:42 really says: "And they devoted themselves to the apostles' teaching and [the] fellowship." Here was a new and different sort of fellowship, which stood out by itself not as *a* fellowship, but as *the* fellowship.

There is perhaps no one place where modern church life is further from that of the New Testament church than right at this point. We speak much of fellowship, and continually tell each other, "What we need is more fellowship." We have youth fellowships, adult fellowships, men's fellowships, fellowship suppers, and other means of seeking to promote a fellow feeling among ourselves. Most of these, however, are efforts to create fellowship on the horizontal level of man's relation to man, and leave out the vertical dimension of man's relation to God. They are often the mere importation into a church setting of the sort of fellowship men seek in service clubs or social gatherings or fraternal organizations. These may help to satisfy the natural desire for social companionship, but as mere human organizations they fall far short of what the New Testament means by fellowship, and are powerless to repair the broken relationships between men.

The fellowship about which the New Testament speaks is the expression of a combined vertical-horizontal relationship. It is the sharing with others of what one shares with Christ. To belong to Christ is to belong to everyone else who belongs to Christ. In the body of Christ, therefore, although there are many differences, there are no distinctions. Christian fellowship is sharing with others the new life which has come to us through the resurrection of Christ. It is to relate ourselves to others as God has related Himself to us. It is to carry over into human relationships the amazing oneness which we have found with God in Christ. "That which we have seen and heard," wrote John, "we proclaim also to you, so that you may have fellowship with us; and our fellowship is with the Father and with his Son Jesus Christ." (1 John 1:3.) To be related to my fellow man as I am related to God—this is Christian fellowship. The shared life of God in the community of faith—nothing short of this is worthy of the church.

This idea is further developed in the New Testament conception of the company of believers as the "household" or "family" of God. Jesus said that all who believed were in His family—they were His brothers, His sisters, His mother. (Mark 3:33-35.) To belong to Him, therefore, means to be a member of a family, to be a brother to everyone else who belongs to Him. The term "brother" became the widely used description for fellow Christians. And Jesus insisted that the ties which united men in the family of faith were deeper and stronger than the ties of earthly kinship. One might have to forsake "brothers or sisters or mother or father or children" for His sake. (Mark 10: 29-30.) Membership in the family of God went beyond the claims of human kinship. It drew men out of the isolation of family, class, caste, race, nation, and united them into one universal brotherhood. All natural barriers were overcome. The only thing that Christians could see in another was that he was a man for whom Christ had died. To be identified with Christ was to be identified with all whom Christ loves.

It immediately becomes clear that this is the only sort of fellowship which can overcome the barriers which men have erected against each other. The broken relationships symbolized by Babel can only be restored in the church. And that is precisely what happened at Pentecost. At Babel the original unity was broken. Men who heretofore had understood each other began to speak in different tongues. Communication between man and man and group and group broke down. Fellowship was fractured. Isolated groups set themselves off from the rest of mankind behind impenetrable barriers. But at Pentecost, exactly the reverse was true. Men "from every nation under heaven . . . heard them speaking in their own language." (See Acts 2:5-6.) Barriers erected by differences of tongue, race, nation, class, and sex were obliterated—proselytes from the Gentiles were included —and the whole group were immediately brought together by two great facts. First, they were all under the judgment of God for the crucifixion of Jesus. Second, they were the objects of God's mercy through the resurrection of Jesus. Nothing else mattered. These representatives from the four corners of the earth were united by standing under God's judgment and His grace.

This fellowship, of course, at that time was among Jews and Jewish proselytes alone. But before long it became clear that what had united the former members of the old Israel into the fellowship of Christ's body was meant to unite all men in the same way. Stephen, in his great defense before his accusers, insisted that God's concern for men could not be limited to the Jews alone. (See Acts 7:2, 9, 30, 44, 48.) Soon Philip took the gospel to the Samaritans. (Acts 8:4-25.) Shortly thereafter Peter went to the home of Cornelius to announce the good news of Jesus to him and his friends, and "the believers from among the circumcised who came with Peter were amazed, because the gift of the Holy Spirit had been poured out even on the Gentiles." (Acts 10:45.) The rift between Jew and Gentile was perhaps as wide and deep as any in human history. Yet this breach was repaired and Jew and Gentile were reconciled to each other, because through Christ they were reconciled to God. Such is the Christian fellowship. It crosses all barriers of age, social status, nation, race, and interest, creating one body in Christ, a fellowship of men who belong to each other by unbreakable ties for no other reason than that they are "equally condemned and equally forgiven sinners."

Service

One other aspect of the life of the church brought into being at Pentecost was a spontaneous outflow of service to others. "All who believed were together and had all things in common; and they sold their possessions and goods and distributed them to all, as any had need." (Acts 2:44-45.) Belonging to each other took the very practical form of serving each other's needs. This was the expression in outward deeds of the quality of life which was in Christ's body. The body shared the life of the Head, who was Jesus. Jesus had accepted as the pattern of His life the Suffering Servant of the Old Testament. Service which was costly was the keynote of His whole career, even to the death. Now, those who shared His life expressed it in a similar desire to serve. The concern of Christ for broken humanity found expression through His body. The church became the embodiment of the Servant, hands and feet to carry into action His concern for men.

The form which their spontaneous concern for the needs of others took was temporary. Economically, the communal life may not have been either successful or desirable. But the concern for others which it manifested is always a mark of the church when it is truly Christ's body. To be in right relations with God is to recognize that all our earthly goods are His gifts to us. It means, further, that these gifts, like the gift of His Spirit, belong to the whole fellowship. We are members of one another even with our material wealth. Selfishly to advance the interests of one member at the expense of another is to violate the wholeness of the body and tends to make it a monstrosity rather than a healthy organism. One of the marks of sharing in the gift of the Spirit on the part of any individual is that he utilizes God's material gifts to him for the good of the whole. To share God's grace is to share His gifts with those in need. To be truly in the fellowship of the Holy Spirit is to number one's self among those who declare voluntarily and gladly that not "any of the things which he possesses is his own." (See Acts 4:32.)

Worship

Worship, too, is a mark of the church's life. They "devoted themselves . . . to the breaking of bread and the prayers." (Acts 2:42.) This feature of their life together, however, will be reserved for fuller study in later chapters. (See chapters 3 and 9.)

Thus the life of Christ in His church expresses itself. Through the unity of reconciled people in the church, through the proclamation of the gospel of reconciliation in Jesus Christ, through the fellowship of redeemed sinners, and through service in Christ's name, the coming Kingdom of God is foreshadowed. These elements of the church's life are imperfectly realized now, but they bear witness to a greater realization yet to come, when all the broken relationships caused by sin shall be restored and God's Kingdom shall come in its fullness.

3

The Historic Roots
of the Church

The church is the heir and fulfillment of Israel. The heart of Israel's creed was given by Jesus to His church as its own: "Hear, O Israel: The Lord our God, the Lord is one; and you shall love the Lord your God with all your heart, and with all your soul, and with all your mind, and with all your strength." (Mark 12:29-30.) Peter referred to Christians as the "elect . . . sojourners of the Dispersion"—an expression which described the old Israel—then proceeded consistently to apply the Old Testament descriptions of Israel to the church. (1 Peter 1:1, A.S.V.; 2:5-10.) The writer to the Hebrews calls the new covenant in Jesus which brought the church into being a covenant with the "house of Israel." (Hebrews 8:8.) Paul called Christians "the true circumcision" (Philippians 3:3), the children of Abraham (Romans 4:16-25), "the commonwealth of Israel" (Ephesians 2:12), and once deliberately termed them "the Israel of God" (Galatians 6:16).

Where the relation of the church to the old Israel is made doubly clear, however, is in Paul's defense before Felix. Paul insisted that Christians worship the same God as Israel ("I worship the God of our fathers"), believe the same Scriptures ("believing everything laid down by the law or written in the prophets"), and share the same hope ("having a hope in God which these themselves accept"). (Acts 24:14-15.) Since, therefore, the church is the fulfillment of the purpose and role of Israel, it is imperative that we examine what that role was, how Israel failed to achieve it, and in what way the new Israel fulfills it.

The Old Covenant

Another name for the Old Testament is the Old Covenant. The New Testament means the New Covenant. This suggests that the things which binds the two Testaments together is the covenant. Note that it is not the *covenant idea* which unites them, but the *covenant itself.* In each instance, the covenant was much more than a mere idea. It was an action, taking place in history, which resulted in a binding relationship between God and His people. The Old Covenant created and sustained the old Israel. The New Covenant created and sustains the new Israel, the church. Both covenants were made by the same God. Both brought into being "God's own people." It is necessary, therefore, to examine the nature of the covenant and its significance for the church.

A Covenant Between Persons

First, the covenant involved the personal dealing of a personal God with a nation of persons. Only persons can make agreements. The covenant, therefore, was not the discovery of certain spiritual laws on the part of the ancient Jews, nor the formulation of a set of religious ideas by men of outstanding religious genius. It was rather the free act of persons entering into a binding agreement in a historic event, which from then on became the decisive factor in the whole course of their history. "All that the Lord *has spoken* we will do," was the people's response when the covenant was made. (Exodus 19:8.) The New Covenant came from "him who *called you,*" said Peter. (1 Peter 2:9.) Ideas and laws do not speak. They cannot be communed with. They do not call. It is only the living, personal God who can confront men with *a word,* and make them hear.

The Covenant Initiated by God

A second element in the covenant relation was that it was established first by God, then received by men. It is not an agreement between equals, a bargain which man struck with the Almighty. Pagan religions surrounding Israel were filled with such ideas of covenant. Their devotees were desperately trying to bring gifts to the gods in order to persuade them to enter into an agreement through which worshipers could escape their wrath or gain their favor. In strong contrast to this, the covenant made with Israel was not one which they had offered to God. It was rather one He had offered to them. God had taken the initiative, and presented the covenant to them. He chose them to be His people before they chose Him to be their God. God had "elected" or appointed them to be His solely by His own free choice. They could accept but could not determine the conditions of the covenant. The conditions were absolute. "Thou shalt" or "thou shalt not" was God's word to them. They could not demand of God in return any "Thou shalt" or "Thou shalt not." They could only accept and obey the conditions, not initiate or bargain or modify them.

The Covenant Grounded in God's Mercy

Again, the covenant was grounded in God's mercy, not in the worthiness nor the achievement of man. To be "elected" was the same as to be "loved." Israel could never claim that because of their number or power or goodness or cleverness they were called to be God's own people. Rather they were the unworthy objects of God's unbelievable love. They were the recipients of "amazing grace." "It was not because you were more in number than any other people that the Lord set his love upon you and chose you, for you were the fewest of all peoples," says Deuteronomy; "but it is because the Lord loves you." (Deuteronomy 7:7-8.) Here was something absolutely unheard of in history. When other gods only terrorized, and when men were feverishly engaging in all sorts of religious ritual and offerings to bribe them into harmlessness, here was a God who called men His own for no other reason than that He loved them. He did not need to be appeased, He did not demand gifts as the price of His beneficence, He did not wait for man to achieve something of worth for which he could be rewarded. He only waited to be gracious, to deal kindly with the undeserving, to show His love to those who were wholly unworthy of it.

God's covenant consisted of an unbelievably gracious act of redemption. "You have seen what I did to the Egyptians, and how I bore you on eagles' wings and brought you to myself"— this was the basis of God's covenant with Israel. (Exodus 19:4.) Love had stepped into history, broken the bands of Egypt's cruelty, and made a people out of those who were no people. It was this overwhelming love of God in delivering His people from bondage at the Exodus which became the center of the preaching of Israel's prophets in all the generations to come. "When Israel was a child, I loved him, and out of Egypt I called my son," said Hosea. (Hosea 11:1.) "You only have I known of all the families of the earth," cried Amos. (Amos 3:2.) "I have loved you with an everlasting love; therefore I have continued my faithfulness to you," said Jeremiah. (Jeremiah 31:3.) It was God's great redemptive act as the expression of His love at the Exodus which forever grounded the covenant in His mercy rather than in man's achievement.

Covenant Demands Response

But love like this demands response. If God in His mercy had brought them out of "the iron furnace" of Egypt, then this laid upon the people whom He had chosen the responsibility to respond to Him when He said: "Listen to my voice, and do all that I command you. So shall you be my people, and I will be your God." (Jeremiah 11:4.) "Election is another name for God's forgiveness." Forgiveness calls out gratitude from the forgiven. Love can be satisfied with nothing less than love in return. And love can never be coerced. It is always free. The covenant made by God, therefore, had to be freely accepted by the people, as token of their glad response to undeserved mercy. "All that the Lord has spoken we will do, and we will be obedient," was the people's part of the covenant relation. (Exodus 24:7.)

Response Involves Responsibility

True response carries with it responsibility. Obedience means not only a docile disposition but the actual carrying out in life of the will of the one who is obeyed. The covenant, therefore, bound together religion and life in a unique way. Religion was life, life was religion. For the covenant was made with a people who were to carry out their response to it in their communal life. The covenant meant a community based on God's will. To serve the God of the covenant, then, was to serve the people of the covenant. A community was created in which there was responsibility to express the will and Lordship of God in every relation. Consequently, the Ten Commandments were given, with their elaboration to specific aspects of behavior (Exodus 19—23), as the norm of the people's responsibility to God and to each other. The law was not a means of gaining God's favor, it was rather a means whereby men could show their gratitude for God's favor. The law was a declaration of God's loving grace to His people. It was His way of showing His people how to live responsibly toward Him and toward their fellow men, that they might know the fullness of life He wanted them to have. The commandments were not so much prohibitions as they were statements of what is not done in covenant relations. They give a picture of the way a man would want to live who was in right relation with God.

In understanding the responsibility of an Israelite to his fellows, it is necessary to recall the Hebrew conception of corporate personality. Our whole education and our patterns of thinking have been directed toward exalting the individual. Because of this we find it difficult to understand the ancient Hebrew's sense of the unity of his people. The whole nation was so much a unit that each individual dwelt in the whole, and the whole dwelt in the individual. When one man sinned, the whole nation sinned. On the other hand, when Israel was saved, each individual shared in that salvation. The unity of the nation was such that the whole group could be designated by an individual name—Israel. It was as though the nation had one soul.

This sense of corporateness may be clearly seen in the story of Achan. All of the booty captured in the destruction of Jericho was to be "devoted" to God—that is, none of it was to be kept, but destroyed as an offering to God. One man, however—Achan —disobeyed God's command, and "took some of the devoted things." Was this merely the sin of this one man? Our individualism would prompt us to say, Yes; if Achan sinned, it was his sin only. But the Biblical writer felt quite otherwise. He tells us that "the *people of Israel* broke faith in regard to the devoted things; for Achan . . . took some . . . and the anger of the Lord burned against the *people of Israel.*" (Joshua 7:1.) The nation was bound into such a solidarity that for one to sin was for all to share in the sin. Achan's sin meant that "*the people of Israel* broke faith." God's anger burned not only against Achan, but "against the people of Israel." We shall see later how precious this conception is, inasmuch as it means that we not only share in the sin of Adam and its consequences, but that by faith in the redemption of Christ we share in its consequences by becoming identified in the corporate reality of the new Adam. But here it is important to understand how this sense of corporateness meant that responsible behavior toward one's fellows was absolutely involved in Israel's response to God's covenant. To wrong a brother was to wrong Israel. To wrong Israel was to wrong the God whose people Israel was. To break community, therefore, by stealing, murdering, lying, committing adultery, was to act irresponsibly toward the covenant, and to fly in the face of the God who in His love had redeemed them.

Responsibility Is Universal

But the covenant not only laid upon the Israelites the responsibility to behave rightly toward their fellows. It also demanded service to those who were outside the covenant community. In order for God to reveal His love to all men, it was necessary first that He reveal His love to some men. If an idea is to survive, it must first be planted. It must take root somewhere, before it can be transplanted or reproduced everywhere. So initially God selected Israel as those to whom His love was to be shown. But did God's love for them mean that He did not love others? No, exactly the opposite was true. He showed them His love so that they in turn could make His love known to *all* men. Abraham, the father of the covenant people, was called in order that in him "all the families of the earth" would be blessed. (Genesis 12:3.) This theme runs throughout the Bible until at the end, in the book of Revelation, the tree of life is growing in full fruit "for the healing of *the nations.*" (Revelation 22:2.)

Election, therefore, is not to privilege but to responsibility. This eliminates all pride in being elected, and destroys all complacency. He who is appointed to know God's love is appointed also to share that love. He who is forgiven must forgive and become an ambassador of forgiveness. He who has known God's loving concern for his own brokenness must share that concern for a broken world. He who has known the joy of membership in the people of God is obligated to seek to extend the bounds of God's people until they take in every life in every land. To accept God's covenant is to labor with Him, to suffer if need be, for that grand hour when "at the name of Jesus every knee should bow, in heaven and on earth and under the earth, and every tongue confess that Jesus Christ is Lord, to the glory of God the Father." (Philippians 2:10-11.) It is to toil and pray and sacrifice to the end that the "kingdom of the world [shall] . . . become the kingdom of our Lord and of his Christ, and he shall reign for ever and ever." (Revelation 11:15.) To accept God's covenant is to serve Him who is the Suffering Servant. To be one of God's beloved sheep whom He calls by name is to go out into the long night with the Great Shepherd searching for those who are lost, "until he finds" them. (Luke 15:3-7.)

Covenant Reinforced Through Worship

Another element in the covenant was worship designed to preserve and reinforce all the other aspects of the covenant. The great problem in any movement is to keep alive the experiences which set it going. The crucial question for Israel was: How could the luster of the faith born at the Exodus be protected from the corrosion of the years? The solution to this problem lay largely in Israel's worship. Worship brought to a focus every element of the covenant.

God commanded His people to erect a tent of worship. This was to remind them constantly that God was in the midst of their life, and was to be a place where they could meet with Him and come to know His will. The instructions were: "Let them make me a sanctuary, that *I may dwell in their midst.*" (Exodus 25:8.) The worship of the tabernacle, therefore, assured the personal dealing of a personal God with His people. The living One was personally present and personally active in the whole of their national life.

Their worship, too, reminded them of God's initiative in redeeming them. Worship, to the Hebrews, was not something which man brought to God on his own. It was rather man's response in gratitude for what God had done and in obedience to what He said. The worship of other peoples could be initiated by men. Men brought what was theirs to appease the anger of the gods, or to bribe them into graciousness, or to bargain with them for their aid in special projects. Worship to the Hebrews, on the other hand, was man's response to what God had done. It was the turning of man to God as the flower turns to the light. It was the rising of man's gratitude and praise as the mountains steam when touched by the sun. The forms of worship were prescribed by God, and even the offerings were first given to man by Him. When life was offered to God in the form of sacrifice, it was not man's gift. It was man's obedient return to God of what He had first given him. (See chapter 9.)

God's mercy, in spite of their unworthiness, was likewise kept before them constantly by their worship. As the deed of their redemption at the Exodus was retold in word and re-enacted in symbol in the Passover Feast, each succeeding generation of Israelites was led to participate in those events anew. They did not think of them as mere memories. They were contemporary events as well. With their conception of the unity of their people, what had happened to their fathers had in a profound sense happened to them. They were there at the Exodus through their solidarity with former generations. And the meaning of the Exodus was to be seen not only in the original deliverance, but in all that flowed from it. Consequently, the first generation which had experienced the original event was also present in their posterity. Joseph had asked that his bones be carried with them at the Exodus as a testimony to the fact that although he was dead, in some way he was participating in that event through his posterity. (Genesis 50:24-25.) Hence, the marvelous kindness of God made known at the Exodus was not just for that one generation, but for the whole of Israel, both past and future. Worship was dramatic action designed to keep their sense of God's goodness and the wonder of His redemption alive in all generations.

Worship was also designed to quicken their response to God and to enforce their responsibility to Him. The motif of the whole book of Exodus is significant in this regard. First came redemption. (Exodus 1—18.) Then followed law, which was a statement of the type of character which redemption demanded from the redeemed. (Exodus 19—23.) Then worship was instituted, not only to remind them of redemption, but to aid in securing and maintaining a character worthy of God's saving act. (Exodus 24—40.) Worship meant the offering of the redeemed soul to God for His service, and the dedication of one's self to the ethical behavior which the covenant demanded.

The communal character of their life was also strengthened through their worship. In other Eastern religions, worship is often an individual matter. The individual goes to his temple to engage in some isolated act of prayer or offering. The worship of the Israelites, however, was corporate. It was a matter for the whole nation. Men, of course, did worship God as individuals, but that was the individualizing of something that was by its very nature corporate. The whole congregation met at the tent of meeting. The feasts were kept by all. Through his worship, the individual Israelite was bound to Israel, past, present, and future. He could worship rightly, therefore, only as he lived in covenant relations to the other members of the covenant community. To break the bonds which tied him to the other members of the fellowship was to sever the bonds which bound him to God. Worship without ethical behavior toward one's brother was an abomination to God. (Isaiah 1:12-17; Jeremiah 22:3-17; Micah 6:6-8; Psalm 51:16-17.)

Worship also focused attention on the covenant demand for service. To be reminded of redemption was likewise to be reminded that they were the heralds of redemption. To recall God's deliverance at the Exodus was to be confronted with the prophetic hope that what He had begun there He would one day complete. Israel had been saved from Egypt in order that she might be God's instrument for one day saving Egypt. "In that day," said one of the prophets, "Israel will be the third with Egypt and Assyria, a blessing in the midst of the earth, whom the Lord of hosts has blessed, saying, 'Blessed be Egypt my people, and Assyria the work of my hands, and Israel my heritage.' " (Isaiah 19:24-25.) The reminder of what God had done, therefore, was also the promise of what God would yet do. Rightly to worship was to serve.

Need for a New Covenant

Such was the meaning of God's covenant with Israel. Here lie the roots of the church. The new Israel was the heir of the old Israel. Her mission was to bring to fulfillment what God had formerly begun. But why was a new Israel necessary? Why did God not complete what He set out to do through the first instrument of His choice?

The answer to these questions lies in Israel's failure to keep the covenant. As the books of Exodus and Numbers clearly show, defection from the covenant followed close upon the heels of the Exodus, even during the wilderness wanderings of the nation. Disloyalty to the covenant grew even worse after they had settled in the Promised Land. Under the courageous leadership of some of the judges, and later such prophets as Elijah and Elisha, the nation was called back to loyalty to the God who had called them into covenant relations with Himself. Recovery of loyalty was only temporary, however, so that it finally became clear to the prophets that God could never achieve what He had set out to do with the nation of Israel. If they themselves would not live in obedience to the God who had called them, they could never be His servants to bring the whole world into obedience to His will.

What then? At first the prophets felt that God's purpose would be achieved through a remnant—a small nucleus of faithful ones within the nation. Judgment would fall on the nation, but a remnant would be spared to carry on Israel's mission. Israel as a nation would have to be bypassed for the Israel of faith—the small group within the nation who loved righteousness and sought to obey God. "Behold, the eyes of the Lord God are upon the sinful kingdom, and I will destroy it from the surface of the ground," cried Amos. (Amos 9:8.) Micah echoed the same note of judgment: "Zion shall be plowed as a field; Jerusalem shall become a heap of ruins." (Micah 3:12.) But both prophets hoped in a surviving remnant as the tool of God's purpose. Amos insisted that God would "not utterly destroy the house of Jacob" (Amos 9:8), and Micah saw that "in the latter days . . . the mountain of the house of the Lord shall be established" (Micah 4:1).

It finally became clear, however, that not even the remnant who survived God's judgment would live in full obedience to the covenant. If the purpose of the covenant were ever to be fulfilled, something new would have to take place to fulfill it at a higher level and in a different form. Jeremiah saw this most clearly. "Behold, the days are coming," he said, "when I will make a *new covenant* with the house of Israel and the house of Judah." (Jeremiah 31:31.) This covenant was not new merely in the sense of being another; it was new also in that it was of a different order. This covenant would not be "like the covenant which I made with their fathers when I took them by the hand to bring them out of the land of Egypt." (Jeremiah 31:32.) That covenant "they broke." The new covenant was to be written "upon their hearts." (Jeremiah 31:33.) Something new was to take place which would change Israel's disobedience into a hearty love of God. An inward transformation was to be wrought at the very core of man's being which should bring him into relationship with God as a son to a father. This would be solely the action of God's grace—a grace mighty enough to accomplish such a change in spite of man's rebellion.

This transformation would result in a new heart that would penitently and gladly accept God's forgiveness of their sin—"I will forgive their iniquity, and I will remember their sin no more." (Jeremiah 31:34.) This forgiveness would be a "new exodus," a new deliverance from a mightier bondage than that of Egypt—the bondage of sin. Gratitude for this mighty deliverance would lead forgiven souls to live in covenant relations with God. At that time God would finally bring into being a people whom He could call His own.

Then He could say without hesitation, "I will be their God, and they shall be my people." (Jeremiah 31:33.) What the Old Covenant had failed to do, the New would accomplish. It was Jesus who brought all this to pass. He made the New Covenant and created the new people of God, the church. It is to a consideration of Him that we shall turn next.

4

The Lord of the Church

The earliest Christian creed consisted of but four words: "Jesus Christ is Lord." (Philippians 2:11.) This has been elaborated in various ways through the long years, but it is still the central Christian belief. The church is made up of those who confess Jesus as Lord. To understand our position in the church, then, it is necessary to face the questions: Who is Jesus? and What does His Lordship involve?

The Apostolic Testimony to Jesus

The answer to these questions must be sought in the New Testament. It contains the only information we have about Jesus. It may seem strange to point this out, but there is no one about whom people are more content to make their judgment on rumor or hearsay than Jesus. The distortions of tradition on the one hand, and the warping influence of present-day patterns of thinking on the other, often obscure the Jesus of the Gospels.

An earlier orthodoxy often gave us a Jesus so remote from anything we know as human that He could never have walked the shores of Galilee or climbed the narrow streets of Capernaum. An effort to correct this has led to the opposite error in our day, at least in the Western world. If the Jesus portrayed in modern art is any clue to what the average man thinks of Him—and it must be, for the pictures sell!—then it is an understatement to say that the Jesus of the Gospels is a stranger to our age. The

modern Jesus has no majesty, no cutting edge, no look of judgment. He has been sentimentalized into a kindly teacher whose
love has no holiness and whose sympathy blinds Him to sin. He
is companion, almost pal, but not Lord. Look at a modern
painting of Jesus, and while doing so recall the lines of one of
Charles Wesley's hymns, and the contrast will be pointed:

> "Jesus, the name high over all,
> In hell, or earth, or sky;
> Angels and men before it fall,
> And devils fear and fly."

The sentimentalized Jesus of our time is not one before whom
men would fall on their faces, and certainly He would frighten
away no devils! He is one whom nobody would crucify, and for
whom few, if any, would be willing to die. He could not have
brought the church into being, nor could He have sustained it
through all the tortuous course of the long centuries.

The Jesus who created the church and whose Spirit gives it
life must be understood in the light of those who were the first
members of the church. The secret of the church's life is *what
the apostles believed and taught about Jesus.* Their communion
with each other was based on their common understanding of
their Lord. The church, said Paul, is "the fellowship of God's
Son, Jesus Christ our Lord" (see 1 Corinthians 1:9), a fellowship
of men based on a mutual faith in the Lordship of Jesus. We
have seen earlier how at Pentecost the fellowship of Christians
within the church is fellowship "with the Father and with his
Son Jesus Christ" (1 John 1:3), and that this mutual communion
is dependent on the testimony of what the apostles had heard,
had seen with their eyes, and had touched with their hands,
concerning Jesus (1 John 1:1). The only fellowship they knew
rested squarely on what they conceived Jesus Christ to be. We
can here mark only the main lines of their belief about Him.

The Pre-existence of Jesus

The first thing of importance to note is that the meaning of
Jesus for the church cannot be understood in the light of His

human career alone. As the visible part of an iceberg is but one-tenth of the total, so the earthly career of Jesus is but a small part of a grand whole. More than nine-tenths of what Jesus is to the church lies hidden beyond the limits of His days on earth. The life of the man Jesus, from the manger in Bethlehem to the Cross of Calvary, is but one chapter in a life which stretches from eternity to eternity. To understand the Teacher of Galilee, there-fore, is to know that He is more than the Teacher of Galilee. To the early church, so simple a thing as Jesus washing His disciples' feet was understood in the light of the fact that "he had come from God and was going to God." (John 13:3.) Before He was born as man, He lived "in the form of God," knowing "equality with God." (Philippians 2:6.) The starting point, then, of the church's faith about Jesus is that He existed before He was born.

The Incarnation of Jesus

Jesus' birth was the point at which this One who had existed from all eternity entered human nature and accepted the limita-tions of a human life. This is what theologians speak of as the Incarnation. This word means "in flesh." At Jesus' birth, the Son of God took on human flesh, and appeared in the world as man. This is the meaning of the story of the Virgin Birth. The marvel is that in this act God became man. Recent attempts have been made to prove the possibility and even the probability of the Virgin Birth by analogies from the field of biology. It is alleged that there are instances where female eggs have produced life without fertilization. Therefore, so runs the argument, Jesus could have been born of a woman without any human father. Such reasoning as this misses the whole point of the story of Jesus' birth. Do these other instances of birth without male fertilization mean that through them God became man? Ob-viously not. The truly significant thing about Jesus' birth, then, is not that He was born of a virgin, but that in His birth of a virgin something happened which never happened before nor since, something unique—namely, God entered human flesh. The earliest use of the doctrine of the Virgin Birth by the Apostolic

Fathers was not to prove that Jesus was divine, but that He was human. The Virgin Birth means that God became man! This can never be proven by any biological theory—nor any theological theory, for that matter. It is the insight of faith. It is not to be proven, but believed. Yet such belief is not blind. It is belief resting upon the testimony of the early church about the One who brought them into being. They could account for their Lord on no grounds other than that His birth in the womb of the virgin was the point at which He who had existed always with God in "light inapproachable" left the glories of the eternal world to visit earth "for us men and for our salvation." This is a stupendous faith, but no faith less than this can account for Jesus nor for His church.

The Life of Jesus

The Gospels tell us practically nothing about Jesus from His birth to His manhood. The early church was not interested in the details of His biography. They were interested rather in those marks in His human life which revealed the divine life behind it. The startling thing, however, is that the marks of Jesus' deity were not the sort of things we would look for in a divine being who had become man. Jesus "emptied himself" of the visible marks of His former divine life. (Philippians 2:7.) The former glory that was His with His Father was now veiled in human flesh. The fact that this man was a visitor from another world was hidden in a life which had all the limitations of other human lives, save sin. Jesus grew weary, hungry, thirsty. He was tempted, He fasted, He prayed, He read the Scriptures, He attended the temple and synagogue services of worship. He thus was fully man in every respect. He completely identified Himself with those whom He had come to save. The writer of Hebrews insists that "he had to be made like his brethren in every respect." (Hebrews 2:17.)

The deity of Jesus is to be seen in His ability to lay aside the marks of His divine life. The most wonderful thing about Him is His restraint, His refusal to step out of the role of man, His complete identification with humankind. This identification was so complete that no human life is too wretched for Jesus to know how he feels and what he endures. Was ever a child born more lowly than He—in a stable? His parents were too poverty-stricken to make a normal offering for Him when they dedicated Him to God. (Luke 2:24; Leviticus 12:8.) His lot in life when He was mature was stated in His own words: "Foxes have holes, and birds of the air have nests; but the Son of man has nowhere to lay his head." (Matthew 8:20.) At the end, He died friendless, condemned as a criminal, buried in a borrowed tomb. When God became man He became wholly man, and endured the bitterest experiences known to man. The divine was hidden in the human. Only the eye of faith could penetrate the veil and find God in the man.

Jesus' Mission as Servant

The symbol of His humiliation which Jesus chose as the pattern of His life was the Suffering Servant of the Old Testament. At this point it may be well to see how the figure of the Servant links Jesus with the covenant discussed in the last chapter. The picture of the Servant in Isaiah seems to be fluid. Sometimes the Servant is presented as the whole nation, Israel. At other times, he seems to be an individual who represents Israel. This fluctuation which seems strange to us is to be understood in the light of the ideas of the covenant and of corporate personality in Israel. Within the covenant, any individual was organically related to the whole nation. Likewise, since the whole nation was so much one that it could bear the name of an individual, as though it had one soul, an individual could be thought of as representing in himself the whole nation.

Jesus brought the corporate and the individual together in Himself. As Servant, He was both an individual and the representative of the whole nation Israel. He so identified Himself with Israel that His perfect obedience to God fulfilled for them the response to the covenant which they had failed to make. Jesus became the new Israel. The combination of the individual and the group idea in the Servant, therefore, made it the fitting picture of Jesus' own mission. This One who had come from heaven where He had lived on "equality with God" was destined later to return to heaven as the "highly exalted" One, with the "name which is above every name." (Philippians 2:9.) But the path from His former glory to His final glory was the pathway of the Servant. Between the two stood the Cross. It is the story of His humiliation which the Gospels tell us, but it must be repeated that this story has meaning only as it is seen in the light of the hidden realities which lie behind it and those which flow from it. It was the early church's faith that Jesus Christ is Lord because Jesus Christ was Suffering Servant. His exaltation to Lordship was not in spite of His humiliation, but because of it.

Jesus' acceptance of the mission of the Servant may be seen clearly at the baptism which inaugurated His public career. There a voice came to His inner consciousness, "Thou art my beloved Son; with thee I am well pleased." (Luke 3:22.) These words are taken right out of the Old Testament, showing that Jesus had been pondering His mission in the light of Scripture. The first half comes from Psalm 2:7. This was a psalm celebrating God's promise to David that he would have a son whose throne would be established forever. Of David's posterity God said: "I will be his father, and he shall be my son." (2 Samuel 7:14.) This decree of God was referred to in Psalm 2:7, where God says of the son of David, "You are my son." The mission of this son was to bring all nations into allegiance to God. "Ask of me, and I will make the nations your heritage, and the ends of the earth your possession." (Psalm 2:8.) It was natural, therefore, that this picture should have come to represent the mission of the Messiah, who as God's anointed would rule the world. For this word to have come to Jesus at the launching of His public career shows that He was consciously embarking on the role of being Israel's Messiah.

But to this word was added a second: "with thee I am well pleased." This was an allusion to the Suffering Servant. Isaiah 42:1 speaks of God's Servant, "in whom my soul delights." For Jesus to hear this word as He embarked on His career as Messiah meant that He was interpreting His messianic mission as that of the Suffering Servant. As the mission of the Messiah in Psalm 2 was to make "the nations" God's heritage, so the mission of the Servant was to "bring forth justice to the nations" (Isaiah 42:1). But how was that mission to be accomplished? It was to be done by a method which would be very discouraging and seemingly a failure. (Isaiah 42:4.) The method was that of suffering. The Servant cries out: "I gave my back to the smiters, and my cheeks to those who pulled out the beard; I hid not my face from shame and spitting." (Isaiah 50:6.) He is described as "despised and rejected by men; a man of sorrows, and acquainted with grief . . . stricken, smitten by God, and afflicted. . . . wounded . . . bruised . . . oppressed . . . put . . . to grief . . . poured out . . . to death." (Isaiah 53:3-12.)

But why all this suffering? Was it merely the consequence of His mission? No, it was the means of His mission. The writer did not mean merely that in being Messiah He would suffer. He meant rather that it was by His very suffering that He became Messiah. It was His suffering for others which became the means of saving others. He "was wounded for our transgressions, he was bruised for our iniquities . . . and the Lord has laid on him the iniquity of us all." (Isaiah 53:5-6.) Although He was absolutely innocent, without any violence or deceit, yet He was slaughtered like a lamb and "cut off out of the land of the living . . . for the transgression of my people." (Isaiah 53:7-8.) The suffering and death of the Servant was not for Himself but for others. By this means He bore the iniquities of sinful Israel so that in spite of their utmost failure to live up to the demands of the covenant, they could "be accounted righteous." (Isaiah 53:11.)

But was this mission of the Servant to be limited to Israel only? No, it was to be the fulfillment of Israel's mission to the whole world. As the covenant had called them to be God's servants to others, so that through them "all the families of the earth will bless themselves" (Genesis 12:3), so the Servant would perform this calling and bring salvation to all. "It is too light a thing," said God, "that you should be my servant to raise up the tribes of Jacob and to restore the preserved of Israel; I will give you as a light to the nations, that my salvation may reach to the end of the earth." (Isaiah 49:6.) The Servant, then, through His suffering and death, was to achieve salvation for all men. Through Him the broken relationships between God and man, and man and man, were to be restored for everyone. The whole tragedy of sin for the whole of humanity was to be overcome by Him.

It was this dreadful, but wonderful, mission on which Jesus embarked at the time of His baptism. Is it any wonder that He was immediately thereafter tempted to divert Himself from this? (Luke 4:1-13.) And is it surprising that this temptation returned again and again to the end? Luke tells us that at the close of the Temptation experience, "the devil . . . departed from him until an opportune time." (Luke 4:13.) Matthew tells us that later on Jesus' disciples tried to turn Him aside from the path of suffering, in which suggestion Jesus heard again the voice of the Tempter. (Matthew 16:23.) The issue was faced to the end, until it reached a climactic struggle in the Garden of Gethsemane. (Mark 14:32-42.)

The decision to fulfill the role of Messiah by suffering was Jesus' own secret from the Baptism to the Great Confession. But as soon as He had led the disciples to confess Him as Messiah, the record tells us: "From that time Jesus began to show his disciples that he must go to Jerusalem and suffer." (Matthew 16:21.) About a week later, as He came down from the Mount of Transfiguration with the inner circle of His disciples, He told them a second time that "the Son of man will suffer." (Matthew 17:12.) Later He spoke similarly to the whole group, "The Son of man is to be delivered into the hands of men, and they will kill him." (Matthew 17:22.) As He led the disciples up to Jerusalem on the last trip, He took them aside from the crowd and secretly reiterated to them: "Behold, we are going up to Jerusalem; and the Son of man will be delivered to the chief priests and scribes, and they will condemn him to death." (Matthew 20:18.) A last time, just two days before His death, Jesus reminded the disciples that "the Son of man will be delivered up to be crucified." (Matthew 26:2.)

The Cross

And then the purpose of His coming was achieved on Good Friday. Abandoned by His disciples and friends, condemned by both Jewish and Roman authorities, mocked by crass soldiers whose eyes were blinded to who He was, lifted up to the ridicule of the world on a cross as a common criminal between thieves, and finally seemingly abandoned even by God, the Servant yielded up His life. He died not because of physical wounds but because of the anguish of rejected love and His holy revulsion against the world's sin. The experience was too much for a human frame to endure. He went out not by the enfeeblement of His body but by the passion of His soul. He finally fulfilled what the prophet had said about the Servant: He "walks in darkness and has no light, yet trusts in the name of the Lord and relies upon his God." (Isaiah 50:10.) In a mystery we shall never understand, He cried out, "My God, my God, why hast thou forsaken me?" yet added, "Father, into thy hands I commit my spirit!" (Mark 15:34; Luke 23:46.)

The Resurrection and Ascension

Had this been the end, the world of course would have been left right where it was, save for one more dastardly deed added to the long roll of man's crimes against God and his fellow man. But resurrection followed crucifixion! The death which seemed to the disciples to be the end of Jesus' mission and their hopes, soon was made known to them as the pathway to glory. It was this final humiliation, this unbelievable condescension, which became the means of Jesus' exaltation. He met His followers who were "looking sad" (Luke 24:17), and said to them: "O foolish men, and slow of heart to believe all that the prophets have spoken! Was it not necessary that the Christ should suffer these things and enter into his glory?" (Luke 24:25-26.) Then He showed them that His suffering was the fulfillment of God's plan to save the world. It was the response of perfect obedience to God at any cost which the old Israel failed to make. It was the fulfillment of "everything written . . . in the law of Moses and the prophets and the psalms." (Luke 24:44.) What God had set out to do in Abraham through the old Israel, He had now done in Jesus as the new Israel.

After resurrection came ascension. The One who had died and risen returned to the glory of His Father to reign with Him. He is now "the ruler of kings on earth." (Revelation 1:5.) Death, resurrection, ascension to the seat of authority—this is what made the early Christians confess that "Jesus Christ is Lord."

It is plain now why the earthly life of Jesus is only a very small part of His whole story. If His career as a Teacher of Galilee were all, then His death was merely a sad confession of failure, one more martyr's death added to the sum total of the world's tragedy, one more eloquent witness to the fact that man destroys the best he knows, one final sealing of our doom. But the Resurrection and Ascension vindicated His death as the means whereby the Suffering Servant had atoned for sin, broken the bonds of death, matched the world's tragedy with a greater and a saving one, and established Himself as Lord of the universe. Since He existed before He came, and lives and rules since He came, His coming meant that God had intervened in human affairs for the salvation of the world.

The Significance of Jesus

The story of Jesus is not the story of a mere man. It is the story of God. The wonder of the Cross is not that a good man died a heroic martyr's death. It is rather that *God is like that!* The One who existed from all eternity, who created the universe, who upholds it by the word of His power, *that One is holy suffering love* as seen in the Cross. And the Resurrection and Ascension demonstrate that this holy love is more than a match for sin. It is victor over it. It has the last word in holding together a world that otherwise had disintegrated. Becoming man, living, suffering, dying, rising, ascending—that is God's answer to a world of broken relationships.

But what does all this mean to the church? It means that *the church lives by all this!* This is the apostolic faith about Jesus. Any faith less than this can never re-create the church in our time nor sustain it. To be in the church, then, is to confess this faith about Jesus, and to own Him as Lord. This means something else, however. It means that *the church lives for this.* As the old Israel was called to be God's witness to the whole world, so the new Israel is likewise called to mission. The words of the risen Christ are plain: "Thus it is written, that the Christ should suffer and on the third day rise from the dead, and that *repentance and forgiveness of sins should be preached in his name to all nations,* beginning from Jerusalem. *You are witnesses* of these things." (Luke 24:46-48.) The church lives *by* the power of the risen Lord through His Spirit. It lives *for* the salvation of the world through the proclamation of Jesus' Lordship.

St. Paul summed up the relation of Jesus to His church in words which cannot be surpassed: May "the God of our Lord Jesus Christ . . . give you spiritual wisdom and the insight to know . . . how tremendous is the power available to us who believe in God. That power is the same divine energy which was demonstrated in Christ when He raised Him from the dead and gave Him the place of supreme honour in heaven—a place that is infinitely superior to any conceivable command, authority, power or control, and which carries with it a Name far beyond any name that could ever be used in this world or the world to come. God has placed everything under the power of Christ and has set Him up as Head of everything for the Church. For the Church is His Body, and in that Body lives fully the One Who fills the whole wide universe." (Ephesians 1:17-23, Phillips' translation.)

5

The Faith of the Church

The church survives by what it believes. It is a fellowship of faith, and by that faith it lives. We have seen that the church is not a sociological fact to be accounted for on any human terms. It is not a human association of like-minded people banded together for self-improvement or social betterment. It is rather a divine fellowship whose life is drawn from Christ. The church lives only because Jesus lives, and because His life flows into it and through it. It is kept alive, therefore, by what it believes about Jesus. It is sustained by all that is involved in its basic confession: Jesus Christ is Lord. Let us examine what the implications of His Lordship are for the faith of the church.

The Exclusiveness of Jesus' Lordship

If Jesus is Lord, He can brook no rivals. The very name "Lord" implies that He is "ruler," "one who has authority." Therefore, all others are His subjects. But this thought in the New Testament goes much beyond the mere meaning of the title itself. The early Christians poured unique content into the title "Lord" when they used it of Jesus. The meaning of this title for the Christians must be drawn from the Old Testament. The very heart of the Old Testament faith was this: "Hear, O Israel: The Lord our God is one Lord." (Deuteronomy 6:4.) The basis on which the faith of Israel rested was that *there is but one God, and that God is absolute ruler of the universe.* Men and nations, the forces of nature, and whatever spiritual powers there may be in the universe around us—all are ruled by Him and subject to His authority. Since there is but one Lord, He is Lord of *all*. The nations are His "heritage," the ends of the earth are His "possession." (Psalm 2:8.)

Now the amazing thing about the early Christians is that they transferred to Jesus all that as Jews they had believed about God. Paul, for example, quotes an Old Testament passage which speaks of God and dares to apply it to Jesus. Referring to Joel 2:32, he writes: "Every one who calls upon the name of the Lord will be saved." (Romans 10:13.) But how is one saved? Paul adds: "If you confess . . . that Jesus is Lord . . . you will be saved." (Romans 10:9.) Calling upon Jesus as Lord was the same thing as calling upon God as Lord. It is obvious, therefore, that all that Paul expected from God he expected from Jesus. The Lordship of Jesus over the world was as absolute as the Lordship of God.

If this be true, certain implications inescapably follow. For one thing, Jesus demands from men not admiration, sympathy, interest, approval; He demands surrender. To be a Christian is first of all to "bow the knee" to Jesus, to "crown Him Lord of all." Friend He was to the early Christians, as well as Counselor, Example, Guide. But before all this He was absolute Lord. "For the Lord our God the Almighty reigns" was the theme song of the early church. (Revelation 19:6.)

It has been pointed out that in this sense Christianity is not a democracy but a monarchy. And it is not a constitutional monarchy, wherein subject and ruler agree on the limits of the rule. It is an absolute monarchy. Men are subject to Him not by a compact they have made with Him, but because they belong to Him. His Lordship, of course, is limited by His righteousness and His holy love. It is not arbitrary, for it is exercised as an expression of His gracious nature. But that gracious nature is not of our choice, and His kindness is not the result of an agreement which we have forced on Him. It is the free exercise of His own nature. We are the beneficiaries of this, but are in no sense responsible for it. He reigns over us absolutely by virtue of His Lordship. It is our source of blessing that His Lordship is gracious. The church confronts the world, then, not primarily with an offer to heal its ills or solve its problems. Its first appeal is to rebels who have taken up arms against their Creator, an appeal which is nothing less than the demand for surrender. The gospel "faces the world with terms, and does not simply suffuse it with a glow." (P. T. Forsyth.)

Another implication of Christ's absolute Lordship is that there is no other way of salvation for man than surrender to Jesus. In this sense, Christianity is absolutely intolerant. Both Old and New Testaments are clear at this point. "For I am God, and there is no other," cries the prophet. (Isaiah 45:22.) What then? The conclusion is inevitable. "Turn to me and be saved, all the ends of the earth!" (Isaiah 45:22.) If there is no God but one, then He is the God of all men, and there can be salvation in no other. The New Testament echoes this same uncompromising truth, save that it sees that the salvation of the one God is now made known in Jesus. Speaking of Jesus, Peter said in his second sermon recorded in the book of the Acts, "And there is salvation in no one else, for there is no other name under heaven given among men by which we must be saved." (Acts 4:12.)

This absoluteness of the Christian faith has long been a stumbling block to many. This is the "scandal" of our faith. How can the narrow stream of holy history recorded in the Bible, the history of a comparatively obscure and insignificant people, a history which to the secular historian is quite unimportant—how, it is asked, can this story have final meaning for the world? How can the salvation of all men in all ages rest on the death of an obscure peasant in a remote corner of the earth nearly two thousand years ago? This is the "offense" of the Christian faith. But offensive or not, *it is the faith of the church!*

Christ does not merely add something to the sum total of the world's knowledge. He is not merely the crown of an evolving process of enlightenment. He is not just the capstone to be placed upon the pillar of other religious faiths. Christ does not supplement other religions, He supplants them. This is not to say, of course, that there is no value in other religions, nor that the church is to despise or treat with contempt the best insights which others have discovered. In the sense of graciousness toward members of other faiths, Christianity by its nature is the most tolerant of all religions. It brings itself under the judgment of its Lord along with others, and lives in penitence for its own failure fully to own Christ's Lordship. It never coerces. It never seeks to propagate itself by means other than those of moral suasion. It survives by its witness to the truth, and by its moral power. As a theological student has recently written, Christianity approaches other religions "not with a faith that confuses politics with its message, nor with a faith that finds its strength in logical argumentation 'proving' its superiority to [them], but with the joy, the purity, and the redemption that the Gospel of the Resurrection holds out to all men."

Should the church grow proud and haughty, should self-will creep into its proclamation, it would thereby make an idol of itself, and thus deny the Lordship of Christ in its own life. But as to its message, it is absolutely intolerant and adamant. It claims the whole world for its Lord. It proclaims that all other efforts at salvation are vain. It does not pronounce on the fate of those who have never known Christ. It leaves them to the mercy of a gracious God in whose love their destiny lies. But it does insist without apology that if such are saved at last, it will be by Christ.

But why should this be considered blameworthy? If God has done a unique thing in Jesus Christ for all men, without which they are left in hopelessness and despair, is it the mark of pride and unworthy intolerance to tell them of this? If one should be caught in a crowded burning building with many doors, only one of which would open, would he be considered a bigot to proclaim to the desperate people with all the force at his command which door would open to their touch and lead them to safety? On the contrary, if he should hold his silence he would be blameworthy! Thus it is with the Christian proclamation. If Christians were proclaiming themselves, or proudly insisting that something which they had devised was superior to all other religious devices, this would be despicable. But the church does not proclaim itself, nor any way of life it has discovered, nor any achievement of its own which it feels is superior to that of others. The church proclaims that God, who by virtue of His creation is Lord of all men, has come to men in Jesus not only to show them that, though they are rebels, He still loves them, but also to offer them the way of escape from the human dilemma, to lift the mark of death on all things human. Is the church selfish to proclaim this? On the other hand, would it not be the supreme selfishness to fail to shout it from the housetops?

The Inclusiveness of Jesus' Lordship

If Jesus' Lordship is exclusive in that it supplants all other lordships, it is inclusive in that it covers the whole of life. It is the church's faith that Jesus is Lord of every aspect of human existence. To the Christian, religion is not a part of life—*it is life.* The whole of life is transformed by Christ. The "mind" is to be renewed by Christ. (Romans 12:2.) The will is to be subdued and relieved of its folly by "understand[ing] what the will of the Lord is." (Ephesians 5:17.) The feelings, too, are to be cleansed. "I beseech you . . . to abstain from the passions of the flesh that wage war against your soul . . . so as to live for the rest of the time in the flesh no longer by human passions but by the will of God." (1 Peter 2:11; 4:2.) Every element of individual behavior is to be brought under the white light of God's will and purpose. "And whatever you do, in word or deed, do everything in the name of the Lord Jesus." (Colossians 3:17.)

But the corporate life of society is also to be brought under the Lordship of Jesus. His will is to prevail in every social relationship of life. Strong though natural family ties are, Jesus sets men into a larger family, the "household of faith," "the household of God" (Galatians 6:10; Ephesians 2:19), the family over which He is Lord. Since His Lordship is absolute, the demands of family kinship must be denied when they conflict with loyalty to Him. "If any one," said Jesus, "comes to me and does not hate his own father and mother and wife and children and brothers and sisters, yes, and even his own life, he cannot be my disciple." (Luke 14:26. Obviously the word "hate" here on the lips of Jesus is not to be taken literally, but is an Oriental form of speech indicating the renunciation of anything which would conflict with the claims of God.)

Furthermore, strong though the bonds are which tie men to their nation, loyalty to Christ must take precedence over patriotism. For "our commonwealth is in heaven." (Philippians 3:20.) Although we are of necessity members of one nation or another, yet in reality we can never be content with any citizenship on earth. Life for us is "the time of our exile." (See 1 Peter 1:17.) Christians are "strangers and exiles on the earth . . . seeking a homeland." (Hebrews 11:13-14.) Final sovereignty, therefore, can never be given to any earthly government. Christ is "the ruler of kings on earth" (Revelation 1:5), and loyalty to Him must take precedence over the claims of any earthly authority. One of the most difficult problems the church faces in every generation is how to relate the limited allegiance it owes to earthly states to the absolute allegiance which belongs to Christ. But throughout the generations, when these two loyalties have clashed, the church has again and again proclaimed with its blood the Lordship of Christ over all of life.

All other aspects of society's life must likewise be brought into subjection to Christ. The claims of race must yield to His Lordship. The fact that one is a member of a particular race is less important to the Christian than that he is a member of the body of Christ. The artificial distinctions between men created by such things as wealth, social position, sex, educational privilege, possession of power through position, must be mastered by Him who "emptied himself, taking the form of a servant." (Philippians 2:7.) To accept Christ's Lordship is to renounce all other lordships. All status which accrues from any attachments other than to Him must be sacrificed. This could not have been put in clearer terms than those used by Jesus: "Whoever of you does not renounce all that he has [not only things, but status, earthly securities, and desires] cannot be my disciple." (Luke 14:33.) If Christ is Lord, and the only Lord, and Lord of all, then the fundamental oneness of those who accept His Lordship transcends all the superficial distinctions among men. These are all made subservient to Him who "is our peace, who has made us both one, and has broken down the dividing wall of hostility . . . that he might create in himself one new man . . . and might reconcile us both to God in one body through the cross, thereby bringing the hostility to an end." (Ephesians 2:14-16.)

The Reality of Jesus' Lordship

Jesus' Lordship lies in the realm of fact, not of theory. It is a matter of history, not of idea. For one to be Lord does not mean for him to discuss or confer about the idea of lordship, and to persuade people in their minds that his rule is a good thing. It is rather to meet men with terms to be accepted, which if not accepted must be established by action. Lordship is an achievement, not an idea. It is a reality, not a thought.

Few aspects of the Christian faith are more misunderstood by both its adherents and its enemies than this. Christianity is not a way of looking at life—a philosophy. It is not a way of living— an ethic. It is not a set of ideas about God—a theology. It involves all these but it is basically other than these. It is an *event,* a *deed,* an *accomplishment,* a *victory.* Speaking of His own work, Jesus said, "No one can enter a strong man's house and plunder his goods, unless he first binds the strong man; then indeed he may plunder his house." (Mark 3:27.) In order to establish His Lordship, therefore, it was necessary that "the ruler of this world be cast out." (John 12:31.) And that was not done by conference. It was done by costly action on a cross. The gospel is the "good news" that *God has acted on behalf of men, to deliver them from the power of sin and death.* By this action, man is set in a new relation to God, to himself, and to his fellow man. Instead of being an enemy of God, he becomes "reconciled to God by the death of his Son." (Romans 5:10.) As for himself, he "has passed from death to life." (John 5:24; 1 John 3:14.) "Fellowship with one another" expressed in "love . . . in deed and in truth" is his relationship to his fellow men. (1 John 1:7; 3:18.) These are not mere ideas. There are things which happen, and are made true only by happening.

It is clear that the belief that God had done something in

Christ "for us men and for our salvation" was the heart of the faith of the early church. In spite of all differences of viewpoint and approach, all the New Testament leaders were in agreement concerning the central facts of their faith. This may be seen in the statement of Paul in 1 Corinthians 15:3ff.: "For I delivered to you as of first importance what I also received, that Christ died for our sins in accordance with the scriptures, that he was buried, that he was raised on the third day in accordance with the scriptures, and that he appeared to Cephas, then to the twelve. Then he appeared to more . . ." A few verses later he speaks of the fact that Christ's resurrection was "the first fruits" of a resurrection in which all "who belong to Christ" are to participate "at his coming." (1 Corinthians 15:23.)

Here is the heart of the Christian faith. Paul insists that this was in no way an individual summary, a "slant" of his own. This he had "received" from the other apostles. He held this in common with them all. "Whether then it was I or they, so we preach and so you believed." (1 Corinthians 15:11.) And what was it that they held in common? It was that the gospel was the proclamation of a series of events wrought by God in Jesus Christ in behalf of man. Although Paul does not say it here, he implies what he says elsewhere, that Jesus was born as a "descend[ant] from David according to the flesh." (See Romans 1:3.) His coming into the world "in accordance with the scriptures" (1 Corinthians 15:3) meant that the prophecies of the Old Testament were fulfilled in Him, and that the New Age toward which the prophets were pointing had been inaugurated. This One who brought the New Age did it by dying for our sins, by rising on the third day, and by ascending to the right hand of God, where He now reigns in exaltation "far above all rule and authority and power and dominion, and above every name that is named, not only in this age but also in that which is to come." (Ephesians 1:20-21.) But there is one other element in the proclamation— He will come again to "bring to light the things now hidden in darkness" and to "disclose the purposes of the heart." (1 Corinthians 4:5.) This summary represents the central affirmation of the early church, the "good news" which they all believed, which had brought the church into being and by which its life was nurtured. And it all involves the simple affirmation that *something wonderful has happened!* It is neither theology, philosophy, nor ethics. It is a simple story of facts. Christ is Lord because these facts are true.

The presentation of these facts, however, always demands a response on the part of the hearer. If God has done something for us, we must accept it. Hence, the proclamation of the "good news" always ended in an appeal for decision. "Repent," was Peter's call at Pentecost, "and be baptized every one of you in the name of Jesus Christ for the forgiveness of your sins." (Acts 2:38.) And when Paul was summing up his career before King Agrippa, he said that he had "declared first to those at Damascus, then at Jerusalem and throughout all the country of Judea, and also to the Gentiles, that they should repent and turn to God and perform deeds worthy of their repentance." (Acts 26:20.) So, whether to Jew or Gentile, the proclamation of the gospel confronted men with the gracious act of God in their behalf, and demanded decision. Since God's action was deliverance from sin, to accept it meant to turn away from sin and to believe in what God had done.

When, however, through repentance and faith one enters the community of the repentant and the faithful, and becomes a member of the "people of God," his new life must be worked out in every relationship. His own mind, feelings, and will must be brought into conformity to his new life, as well as all of his relationships to his fellow men and his world. This means that although the gospel is not a philosophy nor a theology nor an ethic, it involves philosophy, theology, and ethics. The whole of life must be bent to the summons: "Work out your own salvation with fear and trembling; for God is at work in you, both to will and to work for his good pleasure." (Philippians 2:12-13.) Study, struggle, discipline, costly adventure—these are all necessary in trying to discover what the "good pleasure" of God is in every phase of individual and corporate life.

Hence, the Christian never attains, but is always "press[ing] on toward the goal for the prize of the upward call of God in

Christ Jesus." (Philippians 3:14.) He is ever striving toward "mature manhood, to the measure of the stature of the fullness of Christ" (Ephesians 4:13), so that his "manner of life" may "be worthy of the gospel of Christ" (Philippians 1:27). A lifetime is not sufficient to work out all the implications for life of the simple facts of God's gracious action in our behalf in Christ. But these implications are not the faith, they are its expression. It has been said that "by their fruits ye shall *know*" Christians, but not *produce* them. (See Matthew 7:20.) They are produced only by faith in the redemptive events. Christian behavior is the outgrowth of Christian faith.

The Final Manifestation of Jesus' Lordship

One aspect of the church's faith has been largely blotted out for the average Christian in our day—the final victory of Christ at His final appearing. It has become fashionable to say that one is so much interested in Jesus' first coming that he has no interest in His second coming. Furthermore, many have avoided the doctrine of the second coming because of the excesses of those who have lifted it out of its Biblical perspective and have tried to predict events and determine dates. It is true that an abundance of folly has been perpetrated on the world in the name of the second coming of Christ. But the perversion of a doctrine is no justification for its abandonment. The fact remains that the reappearing of Christ is too deeply imbedded in the New Testament records to remove it without hopelessly mutilating them.

The New Testament church lived in tension. Much as the early Christians believed in the glory of what Christ *had done,* they lived in hope of something He was *yet to do.* That which He had begun He would complete. Faith in what He had already accomplished in His first appearing, therefore, quickened hope in what He would do at His final appearing. Jesus was not only the fulfillment of promise, He was also the promise of fulfillment. His Lordship in which the church believed was now hidden, seen only by the eyes of faith. Since this Lordship was real, it must some day be openly manifested for all to see. What is true in the heavenly places where Christ is seated at the right hand of God must become true in the whole created universe which is in rebellion against Him.

At no point is the New Testament more strange to our ears than in this respect. It tells us that "the kingdom of God has come upon" us (Matthew 12:28), yet counsels us to pray, "Thy kingdom come" (Matthew 6:10). It tells us that God has said to Jesus, "Sit at my right hand, till I make thy enemies a stool for thy feet." (Hebrews 1:13.) In this passage the seeming contradiction is clear. To sit at God's right hand meant that Jesus was already Lord. And yet, He is to sit there to await the time when through the subduing of His enemies He will be Lord. It was almost like saying, "Be Lord, until you have become Lord." It was out of this seeming contradiction that the deathless hope of the early Christians was born. Tension between what had already happened and what was yet to happen marked their faith. Their gospel involved what God had done, what He was now doing, and what He would yet do. Living in the present, their faith turned to the past, and their hope to the future.

They felt that at the Cross and the Resurrection, the decisive victory in God's conflict with evil was won. There Jesus was manifested as Lord. But the war is not yet ended. The struggle continues. Because the decisive battle has ended in victory, however, there is no question that the final outcome will be complete victory for Jesus. *He will complete what He has begun!* The hope of the second coming is not only the hope of His appearing. It is the hope of what He will accomplish when He appears. There will be an "end, when he delivers the kingdom to God the Father after destroying every rule and every authority and power." (1 Corinthians 15:24.)

This victory will be not only the achievement of immortality for individual souls. It will be the final establishment of the people of God, a community of redeemed men who through Christ will finally have reached the purpose for which God created man —perfect fellowship with Himself and with each other. Foretastes of this are given to the church now. The gift of the Holy Spirit is a down payment on the inheritance which awaits us at the end. Something of true fellowship with God and with each other is given to the members of Christ's body. These foretastes suggest the glory that shall be given when God has completed His work in Christ in behalf of men. For this we hope.

This hope has a very practical value. It sustains the church when the going gets hard and when the odds seem insurmountable. In a struggle, men can fight on even to the death if they know that their fight will end in victory. When uncertainty of the outcome creeps in, however, the nerve of action is cut. The church's courage is sustained through the knowledge that she is fighting a battle which is already won. As Luther once remarked, the struggles of the church now are but a part of *the celebration of Christ's victory*. Martyrs could go to their death singing praise to Christ, thus celebrating the fact that even though they died, Jesus Christ is Lord, Lord even of the enemies who put them to death. It is this confidence alone which can sustain the church in our time, which is again put under the Cross, facing enemies who would appear unconquerable were it not for the knowledge that they are already conquered.

The final victory will not come by human striving. It will be the act of God. As the first appearance of Christ came at the end of a long period of waiting and hoping on the part of the Old Testament people of God, but was purely God's act, not man's achievement, so the final appearing will come not as an accomplishment of man, but as the gift of God. The time of the end or the form it will assume are not ours to know. They are God's secret. We could not understand them if told. But the church waits in faith, working through love, with the patience of hope. She lives in the full confidence that Jesus will finally overcome, because she hears Him say, "Be of good cheer, I have overcome the world." (John 16:33.) As God was Lord of the old creation through all the process by which it came into being, so Christ is Lord of the new creation at every stage of its development until the end.

6

The Mission of the Church

What image does this chapter title call to your mind? "Mission . . . ." "Oh, yes," says someone, "foreign missions. The Chinese, you know. But, of course, all the missionaries were driven out of China, so there is no mission there any longer. A shame, isn't it, that missions failed so miserably. But, then, people seldom appreciate what you do for them. Well, our church won't have to send any more money over there now. I used to worry about doing that anyway. There are so many uses for it at home, you know."

"Mission . . . ." "Why, our church supports one of those," says another. "That little hall down in the slum section. Drunks and bums come for coffee and doughnuts, and they have a religious service for them. It's nice to get them in off the street that way. Then, too, that little preacher down there—it's good to have places of that sort for people like him to work. He doesn't have much ability. No background, you know. He could never handle a church like ours."

"Mission . . . ." "I remember when I was just a youngster, there was some sort of mission somewhere away off—Kentucky, maybe it was. I can't remember just where. Somewhere up in the mountains, in backwoods country. I recall so well my mother taking things over to the church to pack in a big barrel to send off to those folks. It was a lot of work, of course, but it was a good way to get our old things cleared out. They pile up so much if you don't go through them and discard some occasionally."

For most of us, descriptions like these express what the word "mission" means. We think of it as a branch of the church, an adjunct to the church, one activity in which the church is engaged, but something quite other than the church itself. We think that mission involves a task for a missionary society, or a few odd souls who go to the ends of the earth, or some second-rate people who cannot work well in what we think of as normal situations. But this is to misunderstand the nature of the church's mission.

Mission is not a special function of a part of the church. It is the whole church in action. It is the body of Christ expressing Christ's concern for the whole world. It is God's people seeking to make all men members of the people of God. Mission is the function for which the church exists. "You are . . . God's own people," said Peter to the church. But why? For what purpose had God made them His own? The answer is plain: *"that you may declare the wonderful deeds of him who called you out of darkness into his marvelous light."* (1 Peter 2:9.) To receive God's kindness in being made a member of His people lays upon everyone the obligation to declare that kindness so that others, too, may become His people. The church is *called out* of the world in order to *go to* the world. "They are *not of the world,"* said Jesus, "even as I am *not of the world. . . .* As thou didst send me *into the world,* so I have sent them *into the world."* (John 17:16, 18.) It is the church's mission to be Christ's action in the world now.

The Necessity of Mission

Mission is necessary to the church's life. As Emil Brunner has said: "The Church exists by mission as fire exists by burning." The church was called into being to serve the world, and when she repudiates her mission the church ceases to be the church.

Mission to the whole world is implied in the central truth of Israel's creed, mentioned in chapter 3. The oneness of God and the Lordship of that God mean that He is the God of all men. And those who know Him are to make Him known. But that which is implied in the belief in one God is very plainly stated again and again in the history of the people of God. Abraham was called to be God's man, that "all the families of the earth" should become God's family. (Genesis 12:3.) In order to shield the tender plant of faith from the chilling winds of paganism, Israel at first had to grow up in isolation. But separation from the world was designed to produce a faith which would be taken back to the world.

In this Israel failed. She grew self-centered instead of missionary-minded. She welcomed Gentiles who sought her faith, but made no vigorous effort to win them. Consequently, the nation had to be forced out into the world through a great captivity of half a century. It was during this captivity that Israel once more came to see with clarity her mission to the whole world. She was to be God's Servant to win the nations unto Him. "It is too light a thing," cried the prophet of the exile, "that you should be my servant to raise up the tribes of Jacob and to restore the preserved of Israel; I will give you as a light to the nations, that my salvation may reach to the end of the earth." (Isaiah 49:6.) The book of Jonah continues this theme, condemning Israel for her complacent unwillingness to share her faith with others, and insisting that her destiny could be fulfilled only as she took her faith to the Gentiles.

But Israel did not hearken to these prophetic voices. Instead, the period between Israel's captivity and the coming of Jesus saw her hardening into a narrow mold of self-centeredness more than ever before. Because, therefore, she abandoned her mission to the world, Israel was doomed. Jesus said of her temple, the symbol of God's presence with her, that not one stone would be left standing. (Matthew 24:2.) The kingdom of God would be taken away from her and given to others. (Matthew 21:43.) "Behold, your house is forsaken and desolate," was Jesus' doom song over Israel. (Matthew 23:38.)

A new Israel was formed by Jesus, whose destiny it was to carry its faith to the ends of the earth. Jesus came to die for the sins of the whole world. John the Revelator heard a song in heaven:

"Worthy art thou . . .
for thou wast slain and by thy blood didst ransom men for
  God
from every tribe and tongue and people and nation,
and hast made them a kingdom and priests to our God."
(Revelation 5:9-10.)

The mission of the church, therefore, is to extend to men of
"every tribe and tongue and people and nation" the glad news of
Jesus' redemptive love for them. The charter of the church was
given by Jesus: "You shall be my *witnesses* in Jerusalem and in
all Judea and Samaria and to the end of the earth." (Acts 1:8.)
Should the new Israel fail in this, she would but repeat the
tragedy of the old Israel. And the fate of the old Israel likewise
would be hers. The church can only be the church as she realizes
that her very life is mission.

The Motive for Mission

But is the mission of the church prompted by sheer duty?
Are we to engage in it simply because we must? No, the motiva-
tion is on a far higher level than that. The motive is many-sided.
Let us examine some of the elements which enter into it.

Love to Christ for what He has done for us is the deepest in-
gredient in the motivation to mission. "We love, because he first
loved us." (1 John 4:19.) To know that we are loved by Christ
reaches deeper into our lives than anything else can. For this love
is wholly undeserved. Others may love us because they see something lovely in us, but He loves us even though He sees nothing
lovely in us. The love of others we may in some degree merit, but
His love is ours even though we have no claim on it whatsoever.
Human love is withheld from the undeserving, even though those
who withhold it are themselves sinful. But Christ's love is freely
offered to the sinning, though He Himself is absolutely holy. Love
like this has no human parallel. And it draws forth a response
which is without human parallel. To be loved like this means to
live for Him who loves us. Paul stated it this way: "The love of

Christ controls us, because we are convinced that one has died
for all . . . And he died for all, that those who live might live no
longer for themselves but for him who for their sake died and
was raised." (2 Corinthians 5:14-15.) Isaac Watts took up Paul's
refrain when he wrote,

> "Love so amazing, so divine,
> Demands my soul, my life, my all."

The Lordship of Christ is another powerful element in mo-
tivating us to mission. If Jesus Christ is Lord, then He is Lord
of all. And those who have owned His Lordship can best demonstrate their loyalty to Him by seeking by all possible means to extend His Lordship both to "earth's remotest bound" and to "the
last syllable of recorded time." Here again we see how broad is
the mission of the church. Instead of being the narrow concern
of a minority within the church, it is the task of every Christian
to extend the Lordship of Christ until it is universally acknowledged. The Lord's Prayer is not the monopoly of a few rare souls.
It is the outcry of the whole church:

> "Thy kingdom come,
> Thy will be done,
> On earth as it is in heaven."

The mission of the whole church is to establish in the whole earth
the reign of Jesus Christ. To accept Christ's Lordship is to engage
in this task.

An understanding of *the meaning of the present moment in
the purpose of God* is also a part of the motive for mission. In the
Bible, history has meaning. It is not an endless series of purpose-
less doings which just happen. It is not a treadmill where events
move fast but actually stand still. History is not like a vehicle
caught in the mud, with motor roaring and wheels spinning but
making no progress. It is the stage on which God is enacting a
great drama which has both a climax and a denouement. The
climax of a play is its highest moment, the apex of the action, the
final end toward which it is progressively moving, the crowning
action beyond which it is impossible to go. But this crowning

action is not always self-evident. It may take place without giving plain evidence that it is the highest element in the drama. The climax, therefore, is often followed by a denouement. This is the last scene which unties the knot, clarifies the issue, and throws clear light on the climax. The denouement sets forth the climax for what it really was, the crowning moment in the whole drama which gives everything else its meaning.

The Cross and Resurrection and Ascension of Jesus form the climax of history. In them, the plot of history reached its goal. No higher moment of history can be reached than took place in them. But the climactic role of those events is not plain for all to see. It can be seen only by faith. The final coming of Jesus will be the denouement, the point at which it will be made plain that history reached its final meaning in Him. We live now in the period of history between the climax and the denouement. In most dramas the denouement follows the climax more quickly than in the drama of history. Why the denouement is so long delayed is known only to God. He is the author of the play, and the time of the end is His secret. But in the meantime, there is a sense in which the church is a part of the denouement. For those who are willing to see it, the very existence of the church makes plain that the end of history was achieved in Jesus. The purpose of the church, then, is to declare in the period between the Cross and the Final Coming of Jesus that the drama of history has reached its climax. There is nothing more to be done by God in history than has been done.

When the denouement makes this plain, there will be nothing even in eternity which will go beyond the Cross. The book of the Revelation tells us that eternity will take its meaning from "a Lamb standing, as though it had been slain." (Revelation 5:6.) The heavenly beings "day and night . . . never cease to sing . . . 'Worthy art thou . . . for thou wast slain.' " (Revelation 4:8; 5:9.) Redeemed mankind, too, "a great multitude which no man could number, from every nation, from all tribes and peoples and tongues, stand . . . before the throne and before the Lamb . . . crying out with a loud voice, 'Salvation belongs to our God who sits upon the throne, and to the Lamb!' " (Revelation 7:9-

10.) The eternal meaning of life and history is in Jesus, slain, risen, ascended, reigning. The church exists now to bear witness before the denouement that all this is so.

Our union with Christ is a further motive for mission. To be a member of Christ's body is to be involved with Him in all His concerns. His love for the whole world must find expression in the church where His Spirit dwells. To belong to Him means to identify ourselves with all with whom He has identified Himself. It has been pointed out that involvement includes both responsibility and liability. The church is to be responsible for all those for whom Jesus assumed responsibility. It is also to accept the costly liability which may result from identification with those for whom Jesus assumed liability at the price of His death.

This involvement with the whole world through our union with Christ is clearly set forth in the picture of the Last Judgment which Jesus gave near the close of His life. When "all the nations" are to be gathered before Him, judgment will be made on the basis of men's relationship to Jesus. But how is this relationship to be determined? It is to be by man's treatment of broken humanity with whom Jesus had identified Himself. "I was hungry and you gave me food," said Jesus. "I was thirsty and you gave me drink, I was a stranger and you welcomed me, I was naked and you clothed me, I was sick and you visited me, I was in prison and you came to me. . . . as you did it to one of the least of these my brethren, you did it to me." (Matthew 25:35-36, 40.) To minister to the wretched is to minister to Jesus, for He has identified Himself with them in their wretchedness. What is true for the wretched is true for all men. The glory and meaning of all human life is that Jesus Christ has become man, and in so doing has made Himself one with all men. If we are one with Him, then in Him we too are identified with all men. This summons the church both to the responsibilities and to the liabilities which are involved in witnessing for Him to all men.

One other motive prompts the mission of the church. That is *our unity with the people of God*. Because, as members of Christ's body, we are one with the whole family of God from the beginning of history to the end of time, our own salvation is not complete until the whole family is united in Christ. As was pointed out in chapter 1, there is no such thing as a "private" salvation for individuals. "For God so loved *the world* that he gave his only Son." (John 3:16.) Christ's redemption was not for a few scattered individuals, it was for the whole human race. The salvation of no individual is complete, therefore, until all others who are to be saved are brought to God through Christ. The "body of Christ" can never come to rest while it is maimed. It can find fulfillment only as it is whole, made whole by all its members being grafted into it by faith in Jesus.

This may be an idea which sounds strange to our modern individualism, but it is a thought with which the Bible is very familiar. When, for example, the author of the Epistle to the Hebrews tells us about the mighty faith of the Old Testament characters, he insists that "apart from us they should not be made perfect." (Hebrews 11:40.) Though they were long since dead, they were somehow involved in what happened to the world in the coming of Christ and the formation of the church. Their involvement in what took place long after their individual lives were lived is to be seen also in the account of the Transfiguration. There Moses and Elijah appeared to discuss with Jesus His coming death in Jerusalem, indicating that this event was necessary in order that their own faith of generations before could be brought to completion. This same truth is to be seen in the book of the Revelation, where we are told that "the souls of those who had been slain for the word of God and for the witness they had borne" were crying out still, "O Sovereign Lord, holy and true, how long . . . ?" (Revelation 6:9-10.) The answer was that they were to "rest a little longer, until the number of their fellow servants and their brethren should be complete . . ." (Revelation 6:11.) Here it is plain that even those who had been so full of faith that they had been martyred were still yearning for the completion of their redemption. Until "the number of . . . their brethren should be complete" they were still incomplete.

This idea that the people of God include those who are yet to believe in Jesus is set forth clearly in a rather strange passage in Acts 18:9-11. Paul was in Corinth, facing a Roman trial through the enmity of the Jews. In a vision one night the Lord told Paul not to fear, but to go on preaching the gospel with vigor. The reason was, "for I have many people in this city." That expression literally means, "for I have *a numerous people* in this city." There were many in that city chosen by God to be members of His people even before the apostle had preached to them. The people of God, therefore, are not only those who have already been identified as such, but all those who to the end of time will respond to the preaching of the gospel. No member of this people in any one age is complete until the whole people of God have been brought together in the fold of Christ. For this reason, the church must carry out her mission to the whole world, as the means of gathering together the people of God.

The Sphere of Mission

To fulfill this mission is a total task. The Great Commission recorded in Matthew 28:19-20 suggests the various fields in which this total task must be carried out. *All nations* are to be discipled to Christ. This means that the church should penetrate every quarter of the globe by every possible means with the message that Jesus Christ is Lord. The conception of "foreign missions" as one arm of the church's witness must be abandoned. It is the church's total mission, not "foreign missions," to go to all the world. No nation is "foreign" to Christ. He is Lord of the world, and all men are His subjects.

The church, therefore, must try to detach her faith from all nationalistic ties. It has been one of the misfortunes of Christian history that Christianity, a religion which grew up in the East, should have become a Western religion in the minds of most Orientals. This was perhaps inevitable, in that the gospel was taken back to the East from the West. But the church was not sufficiently diligent to detach the faith from elements of Western culture which had no meaning for the East and which were not in any sense a part of the faith. The rise of nationalism in the Orient which has revolted against Western Christianity is in some sense a judgment of God on the Western church. In penitence, we must now seek to show that Christianity is a world religion. It is above all attachments to particular States. It belongs to man as man, not man as a citizen of some particular country. It may be that the present hour of judgment on the church in the Orient may eventuate in a new day for the faith, where it shall no longer be a "foreign" faith but shall become domesticated in every land.

The church, too, must dare to believe that Jesus' Lordship rules the day-by-day events of history. It must affirm that His redemptive purpose will be achieved in spite of the ruthlessness of human lords. When men are being plunged into hopelessness by the folly and brutality of human leaders in power, cynicism and despair must be confronted with the faith of the early church. They, a persecuted band of wretched folk, without money, power, political influence, or military might, held firm in their faith, even in death, that Jesus, not Caesar, is Lord. No other faith than that can offer men a deathless hope in our time. This witness to Christ's Lordship may in certain areas of the world be possible now only through the silent witness of a life lived for Him, or the final refusal to disown Him under pressure. The form must be adapted to circumstances. The early church at times went underground. But in one form or another, the church's faith in the Lordship of Christ must be maintained. It is the only possible hope for all nations.

But not only are all nations to be brought under Christ's Lordship, *every area of truth* must be consecrated to Him. The church is commissioned by Christ to teach "all that I have commanded you." (Matthew 28:20.) The wholeness of Christian truth must be maintained in order to conquer a whole world. The mission of the church must be freed from sectarianism. A sect is formed by a group of people who make central one aspect of the whole of Christian doctrine, and magnify it out of proportion to its place in the total structure of faith. It arises from teaching men to observe not "all that I have commanded you," but only a part of it. It tends to make men followers of some religious leader more than of Jesus Christ.

This tendency developed early in the church. At Corinth

there were contentions arising from following one apostolic leader rather than another. Paul wrote with vigor insisting that they "be united in the same mind and the same judgment." (1 Corinthians 1:10.) And concerning which leader was to be followed, he asked: "Is Christ divided? Was Paul crucified for you? Or were you baptized in the name of Paul?" (1 Corinthians 1:13.) Paul rebuked people even for following him in a partisan spirit, instead of following Christ in the wholeness of fellowship with other believers. Partial views of the faith can never achieve total mission. Christ claims all truth. The faith must be proclaimed in its wholeness, and in its relation to the whole of truth. Even philosophy, the arts, science, the humanities, must all be brought under the Lordship of Christ and made to serve His ends, if the mission of the church is to be achieved. All Christians, in whatever vocation, should accept their work as a service to Christ and should try to interpret all phases of life in terms of Christ's Lordship. In Him, said Paul, "are hid all the treasures of wisdom and knowledge." (Colossians 2:3.)

All aspects of broken community, too, must be considered a part of the church's mission. The Great Commission commands that men be baptized "in the name of the Father and of the Son and of the Holy Spirit." Here is to be seen the unity in society which makes up the Godhead. For a God like this to be Lord means that all the ruptured relationships among men are to be restored by bringing all men once more into the fellowship that the Father, Son, and Holy Spirit have with each other. This means that the doctrine of the Trinity is no mere theory, no mere source of argument, no mere test of orthodoxy. If the church really believes it, it forms the basis for social passion. The sinful barriers raised between men by nation, class, race, sex, occupation, education, are to be destroyed at the foot of the Cross. The God who was in Christ reconciling the world to Himself was also reconciling all men to each other. For to be reconciled to God is to know a God who in His own Person is a social unity, a fellowship of Persons, distinct yet one. His Lordship will finally create a fellowship of men who, though they are distinct, will truly be one. It is to this end that the church must labor.

The Dynamic for Mission

But all that has been said about the mission of the church is sheer impossibility from the human standpoint. Where shall strength be found to do this, or even to approximate it? It is only through His presence in the church that the task can be faced or discharged. Power lies in His absolute claim: "All authority in heaven and on earth has been given to me." If this is true, then the church goes forth to mission with the highest authority in the universe behind it. And will His authority be given to the church as she labors for Him? We have His own word for it: "Lo, I am with you always, to the close of the age." If the church fares forth to mission without His presence, it is doomed. If it goes at His command and in His strength, it shall conquer though it die.

7

The Form of the Church

Many times people say to their minister: "I was with you in spirit last Sunday but not present in body." It is kind of them, to say the least, to give the church the benefit of the presence of their disembodied spirits! Suppose everybody in the congregation should decide to be present in spirit but not in body. What a delightful time the minister would have preaching to disembodied spirits! No one would go to sleep. No one would arrive late. No one would interrupt the sermon with a coughing spell. No one would think the service lasted too long.

Furthermore, this would solve many of the church's problems. Disembodied spirits would need no heat in winter, no air cooling in summer, no cushioned pews, no redecorated sanctuary, no educational building, no sexton, no organ, minister of music, choir, or hymnals. All they would need would be a minister to visit them occasionally when their spirits happened to be at home in their bodies rather than in church.

And what a tremendous impact a church of disembodied spirits would make on the world! Its testimony to Christ would be silent, undisturbing, and delightfully other-worldly. It would attack no problems, expose no evils, give no evidence of its presence in the community. And should one be seeking the answer to the deep problem of life, or searching for genuine comfort in bereavement, or battling with vicious doubts, or needing strength to overcome some temptation which had assailed him with overpowering force, he would be left to the empty fellowship of spirits floating around somewhere in the gallery, whose bodies were at home, or on the golf course, or scampering off to the beach for an outing.

The Necessity for Form

The evident absurdity of all this makes it clear that dis-embodied spirits, at least in the order of life in which we now live, are quite unreal and without value. Even a jellyfish has *some* form and substance! Spirit must express itself in visible form before it has any reality or any contribution to make to the ongoing drama of history. The church, therefore, is no dis-embodied spirit. As Christ's body, it is the concrete vehicle through which His Spirit must express itself in history. However spiritual the church may be, it must function now in the realm of time and space through visible means which are quite earthly. The body of Christ must have some historic form, or it ceases to exist. The eternal treasure of the church must be carried in some sort of earthen vessel.

The work of Christ through His church must be done in *this* world. Men must hear the gospel, hence the church must produce an adequately trained ministry. The full meaning of the gospel for life must be made clear to those who believe the gospel, hence a program of Christian education must be provided. Christians must be brought into a fellowship which is more intimate and deep than any known outside of Christ. Provision for public worship and the sharing in common tasks are therefore essential. The unfortunate and needy must be ministered to in the name of Christ, hence orphanages, homes for the aged, hospitals, and schools must be maintained in underprivileged areas. The Lordship of Christ must be acknowledged in business, politics, and social custom. For this purpose Christian laymen are to be produced and encouraged to work toward the establishment of Christ's Lordship in every area of life. If the will of Christ, in even the slightest measure, is to be done on this earth as it is in heaven, the church must be organized in some objective form which can be seen and can manifest itself in the concrete relations in which men live out their daily lives.

Freedom of Form

But although the church must have *some* form, no one form is necessary for its existence. No particular structure of church life is divinely ordained. Just as no one form of the state makes a state, so no one form of the church makes a church. A state is a valid state if it expresses the organized life of a people at any given time. It may be democratic in form, or republican, or a constitutional monarchy, or an absolute monarchy, or a dictatorship. It is not the particular form which makes the state. It is the life of a people expressing itself in any one of a number of forms. This is likewise true of the church. It can never be said that unless the visible form of the church assumes one prescribed pattern, it is not the church. The church exists not by form but by the Holy Spirit. Any form, therefore, which the Holy Spirit can inhabit and to which He may impart the life of Christ, must be accepted as valid for the church. As all forms of life adapt themselves to their environment, so does the life of Christ by His Spirit in the church. The final criterion, therefore, by which to determine what the church is, is not form but the presence of the Holy Spirit.

This is made unmistakably plain in the New Testament. There were many in the early church who insisted that the distinguishing marks of the church lay in certain outward forms. Since the church continued the work of the old Israel, they argued, the form of the old Israel must be preserved in the church. Gentiles must be circumcised and the Jewish law must be kept in order for the church to be the church. In each instance where this question was raised, it was finally settled by insisting that where the Holy Spirit is, there is the church, quite apart from particular forms.

Peter made the first major break with the forms of the old Israel. He baptized Cornelius and the company of Gentiles who had gathered with him. He did it on the basis of the fact that "the Holy Spirit had been poured out even on the Gentiles." (Acts 10:45.) He later defended his action by insisting that since "the Holy Spirit fell on them just as on us at the beginning," it would be "withstand[ing] God" to refuse them baptism. (Acts

11:15, 17.) When the issue was later raised at the Council of Jerusalem, Peter again defended his action by saying that God had given "them the Holy Spirit just as he did to us." (Acts 15:8.) James followed with a speech which made very plain what was implied in this. He said: "Symeon has related how God first visited the Gentiles, *to take out of them a people for his name.*" (Acts 15:14.) It was the presence of the Holy Spirit which authenticated them as members of the new Israel, "a people for his name," even though the forms of the old Israel had been abandoned.

When Paul later took up the battle against insistence on the old forms of Judaism for his Gentile converts, he fell back on the Holy Spirit as the distinctive mark of the church. When his Galatian friends were about to be persuaded that to be Christians they had to be circumcised and keep the law of Moses, he wrote to them: "Let me ask you only this: Did you receive the Spirit by works of the law, or by hearing with faith?" (Galatians 3:2.) To "receive the Spirit" had made them members of the new Israel. To return to the old forms, which were now inadequate channels for carrying the Spirit's life, would be a falling back which would lead to incalculable harm.

It is plain, therefore, that to the apostles the presence of the Holy Spirit was the unquestionable sign that the church was present in any group of people, rather than any particular form of church life. One of the early church fathers of the second century, Irenaeus, caught this emphasis of the New Testament when he said: "Where the Spirit of God is, there is the church and all grace." Form is essential, for spirit must be embodied. But the fact of the Spirit's presence is much more important than the particular form under which that presence is manifested.

The church is in the world to serve God's purposes. It must, therefore, be flexible enough to change its form in whatever way will best serve the interests of its Lord. John Calvin described the church as a holy community which must demonstrate in its life that "God has created the world in order that it might be the theatre of His Glory." Whatever form, therefore, best equips the church to turn the earth into a theatre of God's glory is the form which the church should assume. The Spirit of God cannot be imprisoned in any form. The Head must mold the body, not the body imprison the Head. He must be free to create His own forms in every age and locale. Whatever structure best furthers the church's obedience to her Lord in any place or in any time is that for which the church must seek. Any part of the church, therefore, which exalts its own form to a position of finality and refuses the right of other forms to be called the church, is a sect, no matter how old or how large it may be. It is the gospel, witnessed to by the Holy Spirit, which makes the church—not form or structure.

Insistence upon particular forms is disastrous for two reasons: first, it centers attention at the wrong place. It tends to exalt the external institutions which the Holy Spirit has used as vehicles of the gospel rather than the gospel itself. A church which does this is in grave danger of losing the gospel. Secondly, it fails to be flexible enough to adapt itself to the best means of combating evil in new situations or seizing new opportunities for good. New conditions often demand new strategy. When General Braddock brought his well-trained British troops to fight the American Indians, he led them to slaughter and defeat by refusing to adapt his attack to the necessities of forest warfare in place of the accustomed mass attack in the open. He was warned by those who had had experience in Indian fighting that the time-honored European battle strategy would lead to nothing but disaster. Warnings, however, were in vain, and the general foolishly marched to his death in a plan of battle which had served its day well but was obsolete in the American forests. Likewise, to insist on preserving some time-honored form of church strategy merely because it is ancient, is to invite disaster for the church and possible defeat.

Apostolic Succession

One way whereby attention is shifted from the gospel to the institution which carries it is in the insistence of the so-called "catholic" churches on what is called apostolic succession. To them, that which makes the church the church is the fact that its ministry has come down through the centuries in an unbroken line of institutional succession from the apostles to the present hour. It is argued that the unity of the church depends on the passing down through the centuries of the authority given to the apostles by Christ. This must be maintained in unbroken continuity in order to preserve the church in the world. Any breach, therefore, in this external continuity places those who have made it outside the church. Only those who can trace their lineage directly to the apostles have any right to call themselves the church. Hence, the question whether one is in the church must be answered by asking another question: Is he in a body the authority of whose ministry can be traced back *by external succession* to the apostles? This view is held not only by the Roman Catholic Church and the Greek Orthodox Church (which, incidentally, would unchurch the Roman Church!), but by those in other churches who lay special claim to the title "catholic."

Among other objections to this view, three stand out as decisive. First, this use of the word "catholic" is a contradiction in terms. It is the narrowing of the word in a way which denies its own meaning. The word "catholic" means "general, universal." To use it, therefore, to rule out of the church those to whose corporate life the Holy Spirit has unmistakably been given is to rob it of its essential universal meaning, and place limits upon it which the word itself will not allow. The view of the church held historically by the Reformed Churches gives to the word "catholic" its true meaning. The Westminster Confession of Faith says: "The visible church, which is also catholic or universal . . . consists of all those throughout the world that profess the true religion, together with their children."

In the second place, there can be no such thing as "apostolic succession" in the sense of the passing down of apostolic authority through successive generations. As someone has remarked, those who rely on the original bishops cannot produce them any more than those who rely on the inerrant original manuscripts of the New Testament can produce them. But, even if an unbroken historic succession of bishops could be established, still the case for apostolic succession has not been made. Apostolicity lay in a personal authority, given by virtue of the office of the apostles, which office ended with their death. Later bishops took up some of the functions of the apostles, but not their prerogatives. The apostles could pass on the authority of the gospel which they preached, but not the personal authority which was theirs by virtue of their position as apostles. Furthermore, the church is built on the foundation of the apostles' testimony to Christ, not on their personal authority. In fact, it is doubtful whether even during their lifetime the apostles had any such authority as is now claimed by many who profess to be the direct heirs of that authority.

To take but one example, it is likely that the Council of Jerusalem faced one of the most decisive moments in the history of the apostolic church. The question which was there faced would determine the whole future of the Christian movement. Did a Gentile have to become a Jew by being circumcised before he could be a Christian? The outcome of this would determine whether Christianity was to become a universal religion or remain merely a small Jewish sect.

How was the issue decided? By the exercise of official apostolic authority? Not according to the record. We are told in the book of the Acts that Paul and Barnabas were sent from Antioch to Jerusalem to confer with "the apostles *and the elders.*" (Acts 15:2.) Apparently the elders shared in the authority which would be necessary to decide such a question as this. And then, when the issue was debated, the apostles spoke at length to the entire group, seeking by moral suasion and the force of logic to win them to their view. They did not take it upon themselves to make a pronouncement without consultation. When the decision was finally made, Luke tells us that "it seemed good to the apostles *and the elders, with the whole church.*" (Acts 15:22.) Here there is no arbitrary exercise of authority by virtue of office. The authority which the apostles had was theirs by virtue of their moral authority and their experience and their evident indwelling by the Holy Spirit. By this spiritual authority they won the elders and the whole church to their view. The decision was not that of the apostles alone. It was the decision of the church.

Apostolic authority, therefore, was a prerogative exercised by virtue of their testimony to Christ rather than by virtue of their office. Nor could it be passed on to future generations. The only "apostolic succession" possible or worth having is the succession of the apostles' gospel, and the succession of the Holy Spirit who dwelt in the life of the apostolic church.

The third objection to the "catholic" view which rests catholicity on external succession lies in the failure to understand the nature of the means by which the church's life is created and sustained. The life of Christ breathed into the church by the Holy Spirit at Pentecost was not something which is now ours merely because it has passed through generation after generation of Christians until it has finally reached us. This would mean that Christ was actually two thousand years removed from His church. The church is re-created and sustained at every moment by God's gracious gift of Himself now! When Paul was challenged because his Gentile churches had broken the external continuity with the old Israel, he replied that they were in the unbroken continuity of grace through faith from Abraham down. The church lives now as in the days of Paul, by grace through faith, not by external attachment to a questionable historic continuity. It knows the inner continuity of the Spirit as it is renewed day by day, as was the early church, through the gracious self-giving of God. In that it knows the true apostolic succession. As Luther put it: "The church is supported by the Holy Ghost, not by succession of inheritance. . . . for if that should be of value or conclusive, then . . . Caiaphas, Annas, and the Sadducees were also the true church; for they boasted that they were descended from Aaron."

Ministers and Laymen

Those who make external continuity important and exalt form as the mark of the true church, tend to lay great stress on the relation of the official ministry to the being of the church.

For some of them, the church *is* the ministry. The thought of others strongly tends in that direction. In so far as this is true, the church is less the people of God than it is an official class of ordained men through whom, and through whom alone, the laymen find their relation to the church established. If structure is of the essence of the church, and if the guarantee of the right structure lies in unbroken continuity with the apostles, then it is argued that the ministry is that group which, by the receiving of authority through the laying on of the hands of bishops, really constitutes the church. This view was expressed by one who said that the only valid reason he had for knowing that he was a minister was that he had somewhere at home a piece of paper which the bishop had signed saying this was so! The minister exists, then, in the bishop, and the congregation in the ministry. The difference between clergy and laity is not only one of function, but of status.

There seems to be no Biblical justification for such a position. Even in the Old Testament, the whole nation was the priesthood. At Mount Sinai, when the Ten Commandments were given, God spoke to all the people saying, "You shall be to me *a kingdom of priests* and *a holy nation.*" (Exodus 19:6.) It was only for practical purposes that one group was set aside in Israel as a priestly class. "Behold, I have taken the Levites from among the people of Israel instead of every first-born that opens the womb among the people of Israel. The Levites shall be mine, for all the first-born are mine." (Numbers 3:12-13.) The priestly clan, therefore, was a substitute for the first-born of each family for purposes of order and practical efficiency. But they were representative of the whole nation, whose corporate priesthood functioned through these specially chosen representatives.

In the New Testament, Jesus fulfilled the role of priest. He was the One chosen to represent Israel, and through the sacrifice of Himself to make the final and perfect offering to God for the people. In so doing, He created the new Israel. As the church is indwelt by His Spirit, it fulfills the role of priesthood in the world. Peter could apply the Old Testament description of the old Israel to the church: "You are a chosen race, a royal priesthood, a holy nation, God's own people." (1 Peter 2:9.) The whole church is the priesthood now. Nowhere in the New Testament is the word "priest" used to designate a special class of officials in the church. It is applied only to *all* Christians or to Christ.

The office of priesthood, therefore, is shared by all Christians. Consequently, the official ministry of the church has *no different status* from that of the layman. The difference is one of *function* only. Furthermore, the special function of ministering the Word and administering the sacraments belongs to the ministry only by virtue of the fact that the church has designated them as its representatives in this regard. Apart from practical considerations, there would need to be no order of ministry set aside in the church. But to give men time for prolonged study of the faith in order that they might preach and teach the gospel, and to have order and decorum in services of worship and in the administration of the sacraments, the church ordains ministers to do these things in their name. But this in no way exalts them to a status different from the others.

Anything, therefore, which tends to widen the gap between clergy and laity, and any tendency to think of the clergy as the church to which the laymen belong, is a move away from both the Bible and the Reformation. Such remarks as that one is *"just a layman"* or *"only a layman"* should never be heard on Christian lips. The word "layman" comes from the Greek word *laos,* which is the word used in the New Testament to describe the "people of God." To be a layman, therefore, is to be a member of the people of God. And no higher calling than this is possible. It is as absurd to say that a man is "just a layman" as it would be to say that he is "just a Christian." Clergy and laity alike are members of the whole people of God. A clergyman is one to whom certain functions of the whole group have been delegated by the group to be done in their name. The church does not exist in the clergy. The clergy exist in the church. Their calling, appointment, function, and authority all belong to the whole people of God. When they act it is the people of God acting through them.

Luther put this well when he wrote: "We are all priests, and there is no difference between us; that is to say, we have the same power in respect to the Word and all the sacraments. However, no one may make use of this power except by the consent of the community. . . . For what is the common property of all, no individual may arrogate to himself." To exalt the status of a clergyman above that of the layman is to dishonor the church in whose name and by whose authority the clergyman acts. The clergy are mere servants of the church. If they understand their proper role in the church, they will be seeking to fulfill the high demand of Jesus: "Whoever would be great among you must be your servant . . . even as the Son of man came not to be served but to serve, and to give his life as a ransom for many." (Matthew 20:26, 28.)

On the other hand, the layman must recognize that the minister, by his function in the church, has certain responsibilities of leadership which are to be respected. If a layman is as competent a theologian as a minister, he has as much theological authority in the church as he. But let not the layman who is ignorant of theology set his private opinion up against that of the minister as equally valid. Where the medical layman or the legal layman would not think of encroaching on the field of the medical or legal expert, the theological layman, who cannot possibly give the years to study which is required of the ministry, will ofttimes take it upon himself to pronounce with finality, without recognizing that he may be speaking in a field where he is highly incompetent. If the church assigns special functions to the ministry in their name, it is only wise that the church should give strong heed to the corporate judgment of its ministers in those areas. A lay religion which is theologically uninformed and secularized, or narrowly cramped and traditionalized, may be as disastrous to the church as clericalism.

Having said this, however, it must be reiterated that the current cleavage between ministers and laymen must somehow be overcome. Protestantism cannot live as a clerical religion. When theological thinking and church administration and devout living become the functions of special orders within the church instead of the whole church, Protestantism is on the way out. Far better is it to heed the example of a Protestant group behind the iron curtain who have a lay office corresponding to every clerical office from the top to the bottom of the organized life of the church, and whose chairman of the theological commission of the whole denomination is a layman! An informed visitor there remarked that if every pastor were killed the church would go right on. An interesting touch from the life of the Iona Community in Scotland is suggestive also. There the Communion loaf is passed through the congregation, each member breaking off a piece and giving it to the one sitting next to him, thus signifying that each man is a priest to his neighbor and all are members of the one priesthood of believers. It is only as clergy and laity function together as members of the one people of God that Protestantism can claim the future. Paul summed it up thus: "For as in one body we have many members, and all the members do not have the same function, so we, though many, are one body in Christ, and individually members one of another." (Romans 12:4-5.)

Types of Form

There have been three major types of form which the church has assumed in its history. The first is the episcopal, or monarchic, type. In this type great stress is laid on the historic episcopate, or the continuation of an order of superior clergy—bishops. They are the guardians of tradition, and the final arbiters of authority in the life of the church. For some adherents of this form the historic episcopate is necessary to the existence of the church. "No bishop, no church." For others, it is not absolutely necessary for the being of the church, but is so desirable for the well-being of the church that they can hardly think of a church without bishops.

The second type is presbyterial, or representative. In this type all the clergy are on the same level. Authority is vested in representatives chosen by the people, both ministerial and lay, who act in their name. The local church is governed by the pastor, or pastors if there be more than one, and elders elected by the congregation, who usually outnumber the pastors. At all levels above the local church, the representatives who act for the church are evenly divided between clergy and laymen, thus demonstrating their parity. In the presbyterial system, tradition is not considered valid as a guide to doctrine or practice, but is always subordinated to the Word of God in the Scriptures.

The third type is congregational, or democratic. Like the presbyterial form, the congregational knows only one order of clergy. Authority, however, is not vested in chosen representatives who act for the people, but lies in the direct action of the people themselves. The church exists in the local congregation. It is united with other congregations not organically, but only on the basis of voluntary fellowship, from which the local church may withdraw at any time, and still remain a church. It is believed that the autonomy of the local church permits the direct leadership of the Holy Spirit at each particular place and time.

A fourth type, not widely held, is one in which all possible external form is abandoned in the interests of giving free play to the immediate leadership of the Holy Spirit. The Quakers are representative of this type. The ministry, sacraments, and all stated forms of worship are abandoned. Even the Bible is made secondary to the "inner light," which is believed to be the Holy Spirit's direct and unmediated guidance in the church now.

This fourth type of form has never taken very wide hold of the life of the church, and is not likely ever to do so, inasmuch as it fails to stress sufficiently the fact that in the present world forms are necessary for spirit to express itself. The other three have been widely held throughout Christendom. Apart from the Roman Catholic Church, the presbyterial form, with various modifications, has had the largest number of adherents. The episcopal system is not based on the Scriptures, but on the developing tradition in the early church which, it is argued, grew up under the guidance of the Holy Spirit. The presbyterial and congregational forms both claim Scriptural support. Where the weight of Scripture lies would be quite largely determined by the presuppositions with which one begins his study.

The greatest stumbling block in the way of the unity of the church in our time is the difference of judgment as to the proper form of the church. There is no one place where the churches should lay aside prejudice and listen together for the voice of the Holy Spirit through the Scriptures more than in this area. It is possible that the form which the living church would assume in our day, were it not for the hindering of our sinfulness, would be one which would conserve all the values which the three historic forms champion—the value of true tradition, the authority of the Word of God, and the contemporary experience of the church through the Holy Spirit.

8

The Purity of the Church

"I think I shall have to leave the church," confided a young minister to an older one, "and find somewhere outside it where I may work for Christ. Perhaps schoolteaching would be more fruitful than the pastorate. There, at least, one can work with the unprejudiced minds of children, and hope to mold some of them in patterns of thought which are Christian. But the church—it is too steeped in tradition and too rigid to change!"

This young man was facing a problem which has been faced throughout the centuries—the problem of the church's failure. If the church is the body of Christ, how can Christ have such an imperfect body? And if the church is defective, is it really the body of Christ? Many have wrestled with this problem, and the answer to it is not easy. The issues it involves are very complex. No simple or superficial answer will do. Let us first of all seek to determine the nature of the problem.

The Problem

The church is a paradox, a reality with seemingly contradictory elements. The church is divine, a body in which the Spirit of God Himself lives and acts. And yet the church is human, made up of men who are finite and faulty. The church is spiritual, yet earthly. It is holy, yet it is composed of sinful men. It is at one and the same time the body of Christ and a human institution. It partakes of eternity, with a quality of life which this world can neither produce nor understand, and yet this eternal quality of life must work itself out through the historic forms of the church which are quite tied to this world and subject to all the limitations of time and change. As we saw in the last chapter, the church cannot escape some form of embodiment. It must take shape in *this* world, made up of people, officers, buildings, meetings, tasks, finances. Because of this, it is impossible fully to exclude the world and have a church without any imperfections. All human institutions are limited and imperfect. The church is different from the world, yet in many ways it is quite like the world. The difference between the two, therefore, is not easily marked off in every instance.

But is not this seeming contradiction true of all living things? Life is always in some sort of body. And yet the life is other than the body. Suppose, for example, a person otherwise in perfect health suddenly dies from a blockage in a heart artery. An operation might remove the tissue which caused the blockage. Then, presumably, there would still be a quite perfect body. All the organs would be intact and without disease or defect. But without life, they are useless. It is impossible for life to express itself except through them, and yet they are nothing without life. On the other hand, life may function in a diseased or deformed body, with many of its members cut off and even some of the vital organs badly impaired. One can neither isolate life from the body, nor yet identify the body, particularly in its diseased and deformed parts, with the life.

This is all a parable of a living church. The life of the church is spiritual, yet it expresses itself through earthly institutions. It is divine, but it functions through men. It is holy, yet it works through people who are sinful. In searching for the real church, therefore, we are always faced with the dilemma of trying to isolate it from its faulty historical forms, thus making it a spiritual thing which exists only in some eternal dream world quite apart from the world in which we live, or, on the other hand, of identifying the true church so much with its faulty historic forms that we fail to understand that it is something more than these. We must avoid this dilemma by understanding that both sides of the seeming contradiction must be held together.

The church is both the perfect spiritual life of Christ and its imperfect embodiment in sinful men. Paul could write to the Corinthian Christians, "God's temple is holy, and that temple you are." (1 Corinthians 3:17.) Yet, at the same time, he could rebuke the members of this temple for strife and division, immorality, going to pagan courts against Christian brothers, misuse of the Lord's Supper, spiritual pride in place of love, and a failure to understand the doctrine of the resurrection. With all these defects, the Corinthian group were still the "church . . . at Corinth" to Paul. When he wrote "to the church of God which is at Corinth" (1 Corinthians 1:2), he was not writing to some ideal, disembodied, invisible, spiritual church. He was writing to the flesh and blood members of that church who, with all their defects, were "the church of God" in their corporate life.

It is to be remembered, however, that Paul was not content to do nothing about the defects in the life of the Corinthian church. He could not allow the church to baptize evil, to surrender to the world, and to identify all the diseased elements of its life with that life itself. By instruction, warnings, and exhortations, he urged the Corinthian Christians to deal drastically with the diseased members and cancerous growths which were imperilling the life of the church, and to strive to make the organs of Christ's life holy, even as that life was holy in itself.

Two Questionable Attitudes

Throughout the church's history, the tension between what the church ought to be "in Christ" and what it actually is in its historic life has been acutely felt. Two attitudes have often been taken toward this problem, neither of which has New Testament sanction. The first is that of withdrawal from the organized church. This has been the answer of many small sects who, mindful of the holiness of the church and eager for the renewal of its life, have tried to bring this about by separating themselves and starting movements of their own. This has led to the scandal of having over three hundred different denominations in America at present, with new sects arising nearly every year.

The folly of this is apparent. It is an effort to escape from the weaknesses and sinfulness inherent in the human side of the church's life. But it immediately falls prey to the fact that those who withdraw from the larger life of the church are themselves weak and sinful, and carry with them the very defects which they seek to escape. In almost every instance where this has been tried, the group which has withdrawn has later developed within its own life things which some in the group did not like, so that the separated group itself was split by a new separation. And usually the process of splintering goes on and on. It has been this which partly, at least, has accounted for so many denominations in America.

The second attitude is one which avoids the perils of the first by making peace with the elements of the world in the church's life. It has no cutting edge, makes little challenge to sin within the church, paganizes the body of Christ, and ends up content to have the church nothing more than an organization which lends moral respectability to society. This attitude tends to identify the church that *is* with the church that *ought to be*. It makes peace with a hostile world, throws the garments of sanctity around the status quo, and is quite content to have it so. The first attitude leads to intolerance and bigotry, the second to complacency and compromise. The first errs in trying to detach the life of the church from the body, the second in identifying that life with the body. The first is wrong in thinking that a church can be developed which does not sin, the second in holding that it is all right for the church to sin.

Purity Seen by Faith

Since the church is both earthly and heavenly, both holy and impure at the same time, its absolute holiness can be seen only by faith. If the line between the church and the world were absolutely clear, it would require no faith to see the difference. A worldling could see it as well as a saint. But the church, like salvation, is present to faith. The world can see the failures of the church clearly. So can its members, if they are honest. But the true righteousness of the church, that true holiness which the

Lord of the church is building into it, so that "the church might be presented before him in splendor, without spot or wrinkle or any such thing" (Ephesians 5:27), is to be seen only by the eye of faith.

There are given to the church now some foretastes of this final holiness. But its completion and perfection are present only to faith. We do not *see* that the church is holy, we *believe* it. There are enough signs of this holiness in the life of the church for our faith to lay hold of. Some measure of holiness is present. After listing a number of the grosser sins, Paul could write to the Corinthians, "And such were some of you. But you were washed, you were sanctified." (1 Corinthians 6:9-11.) And yet, as we have already noted, the Corinthian Church was not wholly cleansed by any means. It had enough signs of true holiness to encourage the faith which Paul expressed to another church, that "he who began a good work in you will bring it to completion at the day of Jesus Christ" (Philippians 1:6), and yet it was plagued with many distressing defects. Just as in the case of our personal purity, the purity of the church is more a matter of faith than of sight.

The Church Both Present and Future

The reason the purity of the church can be seen only by faith is because of its strange nature as both a present and a future reality. The church is here, and yet the church is still to come. The true church belongs to what the Bible calls "the age to come." Yet, at Pentecost, this "age to come" broke into this "present age" in the founding of the church. Since Pentecost, therefore, the church is already here but it is here as much in promise as in reality, here more as anticipation than as realization.

The church is a fellowship of hope. It lives in the confidence that the foretastes of holiness which are now given are signs of what the church will finally be when this present age is ended. But the foretastes are given in the midst of sin and weakness. We must live now in all the baffling contradictions of the struggle with evil. The church is never holy in itself. It is holy only *in Christ,* whose final triumph we await. In Romans Paul reminds us that it is the lot of the Christian to "wait." "For in . . . hope we were saved. Now hope that is seen is not hope. For who hopes for what he sees? But if we hope for what we do not see, we wait for it with patience." (Romans 8:24-25.) We see the signs of the church's purity in the cleansed lives of her members, and in her corporate witness to righteousness in the world. But this purity is far from perfect. Its fullness we await with patience.

One of the major errors of the Roman Church lies in a failure to recognize this. To it, the holiness of the church is not future but present. Its purity is not a matter of faith, but of sight. The church is perfect, therefore the church cannot sin. The pope, as head of the church, is infallible in his official pronouncements about the faith. No admixture of human error, no clinging taint of sin, is to be seen in the church. But this view is not confined to the Roman Church entirely. There are many small Protestant sects which cherish a similar error. They feel that their group has achieved purity, that their final holiness is not something they await, but something which is a present possession in all its fullness. This fosters spiritual pride and removes the element of self-judgment from the church. Whether in Roman or Protestant form, this view removes the tension between what the church already is and what it is yet to be. And in so doing, it moves away from the central throb of the New Testament. As with final salvation, so with final purity, the church is that fellowship of saints who

> ". . . see their triumph from afar,
> By *faith* they bring it nigh."

Judgment and Renewal

Since the church is both divine and human, both holy and sinful, it is necessary that it live constantly under the judgment of God in order that it may be purged of its sin and constantly renewed in holiness. Several aspects of this process should be called to mind.

First, the renewal normally *should be made from within the church* rather than by withdrawing from it. It is the testimony of history that most vital movements for the quickening of the life of the church have been efforts to reform it from within rather than to separate from it. Separatist movements rarely make any large or lasting contribution to the life of the whole church. No matter how vital they may be within themselves, they lose their vitalizing function in the whole body by withdrawing from it. Luther never intended to withdraw from the Roman Church; he was forced out. Wesley never did withdraw from the Church of England. His movement was forced out, but he died a minister in good standing in the church of his childhood.

The word "reform" means literally "to form again." The word "Protestant" does not mean to object to something. It comes from the Latin word *protestari,* which means "to witness, to declare publicly." The Protestant Reformation, therefore, was a public declaration of the faith of the apostolic church, an effort to form again the legions of righteousness after they had fallen apart under the pressure of medieval wickedness. It was not an effort to form a new army, but to renew the old army. Splinter groups which by their own choice leave the organized church, usually become rather negative protests in the form of objections more than public witnesses to the faith within the life of the church. And splinters usually are brittle and have rough edges, which tend to make them splinter again and again. "The time has come for judgment to begin with the household of God," said Peter. (1 Peter 4:17.) But let it begin within the household of God, not by withdrawing from it.

In the second place, self-righteousness is ruled out for any who seek the church's renewal, because *we are all responsible for the condition of the church.* So often one hears it said, "Why doesn't the church do so-and-so?" Well, who is the church? For a member of the church to say this is to condemn himself. Either he has done nothing about it himself, or what he has done has not been sufficient to accomplish the ends sought. In either case, he is at least partly to blame. But even if he has done his very best to change things and has failed, still he is so involved in the life of the whole church that he must share its failure. Jeremiah did his best to turn his people from their evil ways, to divert the destruction of the nation, but failed. When, however, the nation was destroyed, and he was offered asylum in Babylon with a pension for life, he refused it, choosing rather to dwell "among the people who were left in the land." (Jeremiah 40:2-6.) He stayed by the movement even when it went down. In our own day, even though Kagawa did all he could to dissuade his country from invading China, when they did it he shared responsibility and wept in penitence. We are so closely bound up with the church that we share both its triumphs and its defeats, we partake of both its holiness and its sin. Our part in the church's renewal, therefore, is not to try to stand outside the situation and point an accusing finger. It is rather to do our part openly in declaring the faith, living in constant penitence, and seeking the grace of God who can form the church's life anew as by a resurrection from the dead.

A third thing to keep in mind is that *judgment belongs to God,* not to us. There are times when God's judgment functions through His church. Christ reigns through His body on earth, and in flagrant cases of open sin which publicly deny the Lord of the church it may be necessary for the church to discipline its members as a part of its testimony to the world. Jesus cleansed the temple. (Matthew 21:12-13.) Peter brought judgment on Ananias and Sapphira. (Acts 5:1-10.) Paul smote Elymas with blindness (Acts 13:6-11), and cast an incestuous man out of the fellowship (1 Corinthians 5:1-2). But these were all clear cases of defection from the faith, and did not involve questions where the judgment of good men might differ. There are areas of behavior, however, where individual liberty must be permitted, and men must be left to the judgment of God. He is the only one who knows the secrets of the heart, who fully understands human motivation, who can take into account all the factors in the complex problems of human behavior. We must often hold men in the fellowship whom we consider weak in faith and whose behavior patterns are disturbing to us.

Paul faced such a situation in the church at Rome. There was difference of opinion there about the proper food for Christians to eat. Some were vegetarians, others felt free to eat meat.

Those who ate meat looked upon the scruples of their brethren as weakness, and called them "weak in faith." Paul wrote to them, "Let not him who eats despise him who abstains, and let not him who abstains pass judgment on him who eats." (Romans 14:1-3.) What was the basis of Paul's counsel here? It was this—"for God has welcomed him." And if God has welcomed a man, "Who are you to pass judgment on the servant of another? It is before his own master that he stands or falls." (Romans 14:4.) Paul further insisted that we should have faith that even the weak will finally be brought into a fuller faith, for he added: "And he will be upheld, for the Master is able to make him stand." (Romans 14:4.) God is both Judge and Sustainer. Our relationship to a weaker brother, therefore, should be less one of censure than of witnessing before him to the deeper aspects of the faith, prayer in his behalf, and faith that God will bring him through.

In viewing our brother, it is imperative that we remember always that God is the final judge. "Why do you pass judgment on your brother? . . . For we shall all stand before the judgment seat of God . . . So each of us shall *give account of himself* to God. Then let us no more pass judgment on one another, but rather decide never to put a stumbling-block or hindrance in the way of a brother." (Romans 14:10-13.) The church finds its renewal by living under God's judgment, by each member taking more care to cast out the log from his own eye than to extract the splinter from the eye of his brother.

Christ and the Church's Purity

One final consideration should be kept in mind. The church belongs to Christ. And in spite of all its weaknesses, defects, and sins, He has not abandoned His church. He judges the church constantly, but always judges in love. If He is willing to abide in His church and to give His Spirit to sinful men, can we do any less than stand by the church as Christ's body, even though that body is often distorted by the sin of men—yes, even by our own sin? "Christ loved the church and gave himself up for her." (Ephesians 5:25.) To Him the church was worth the Cross! And it is through the church that Christ chooses to do His saving work in the world. It is the divine purpose, said Paul, "that through the church the manifold wisdom of God might now be made known to the principalities and powers in the heavenly places." (Ephesians 3:10.) And Jesus intends finally to present the church "before him in splendor, without spot or wrinkle or any such thing, that she might be holy and without blemish." (Ephesians 5:27.)

No one has yet seen the church in all her splendor. Not until time has passed away, and the city of God whose spires lie "beyond the rim of the sky" has come, shall the church be seen in all her glory. Then the saints of all the ages shall have "washed their robes and made them white in the blood of the Lamb." (Revelation 7:14.) When the faithful of all ages, from Adam to the end of time, shall join their voices with the heavenly beings who rest not day nor night, and shall sing, "Hallelujah! . . . for the marriage of the Lamb has come, and his Bride has made herself ready" (Revelation 19:6-7), then the church, which is Christ's Bride, shall stand forth in all her eternal beauty, made glorious with the beauty of Christ's holiness and adorned with the garments of His righteousness. It is for that church that we labor, and love, and hope. Let us within the limitations of the present church wait with patience for the church to come, and be faithful to the end.

9

The Worship of the Church

The voice of the minister rings out clearly: "O come, let us worship and bow down, let us kneel before the Lord, our Maker!" Then all heads are bowed for prayer, after which hymns of praise ascend, the Scriptures are read, an offering is made, and a sermon preached. "O come, let us worship . . ." This is the characteristic note of a gathered congregation, that which sets it off from other human gatherings. Others meet for pleasure, or study, or to plot a course of action. The church meets to worship.

Worship may involve enjoyment, instruction, plans for action —in fact, true worship will almost inevitably include these—but it is more and other than these. That which transforms these into worship is the fact of God, and the relationship of the worshipers to Him. The joy of the worshiper is in God. His instruction is in the will of God. His plans for action are to make God's will prevail in human affairs. The centrality of God is what makes worship worship.

The Meaning of Christian Worship

Although all worship centers in God, Christian worship differs from other worship. The nature of the God who is worshiped determines the meaning of the worship offered to Him. Since the God of the Christian is the God made known in Jesus Christ, the nature of true Christian worship is to be determined by His character and by the relation of men to Him. The central thing

revealed about God through Jesus Christ is that He is a gracious
God who redeems sinful men. This means, therefore, that true
Christian worship is not something man does for God but is
rather the response man makes to what God has already done for
him.

At this point Biblical worship is unique. The forms of worship used by the Hebrews in Old Testament times were in many
respects outwardly similar to the forms of worship used by the
nations around them. They had a tabernacle or temple as a
sacred place, they had a priesthood, they had sacrifices, they made
offerings. So did the other peoples of that day. But as we have
already seen in chapter 3, these others thought of worship as
something man was presenting to God. The gods were angry,
therefore gifts were brought to appease their wrath. Or the gods
controlled the fertility of soil, animals, and men, therefore offerings were made to win their favor. The gods, too, determined the
outcome of battles, therefore efforts were made to bribe the gods
into overcoming rival deities and assuring victory. Attempts were
also made, by ritual and ceremony, by sacred meals and drink
offerings, to enter into communion with the gods so that their
divine life might be implanted in men.

The acts of Hebrew worship paralleled these in many outward respects. The inner meaning of them, however, was vastly
different. The pagans initiated their acts of worship themselves,
in the hope of doing something which would gain the favor of the
gods. Hebrew worship was initiated by God, and was engaged in
by the worshiper only as *a response to what God had already
done for him*. Worship was not designed to gain God's favor. It
was rather the glad recognition that a gracious God had already,
on His own initiative, offered His favor. Even the Hebrew offerings were not something which man gave to God. They were
rather the offering to God of what He had first given them. They
were the answer of man's faith in God's grace. They were a form
of obedience to God's will.

This is made very clear in the book of Leviticus, where blood
offerings for the atonement of sin were specified. The reason for
these sacrificial offerings was this: God said, *"I have given it for*

you upon the altar to make atonement for your souls." (Leviticus 17:11.) Obviously, the worshiper was not giving something to God to win His favor. On the contrary, by making his offerings he was indicating two things: first, that he believed that God was gracious in giving him a means of atoning for his sin; and second, that he was obeying God's will in accepting His provided means of salvation instead of trying to make one of his own. Faith and obedience are really two sides of one reality. Obedience is faith expressing itself in action. Hence, Biblical worship in no sense involved man's offering something to God. It was rather man's obedient response to God in presenting the offering God had given to him, in obedience to His will.

The obedience of faith in Biblical worship is always accompanied by the element of praise and adoration.

"I was glad when they said to me,
   'Let us go to the house of the Lord!' " (Psalm 122:1.)
"O give thanks to the Lord, for he is good;
   his steadfast love endures for ever!" (Psalm 118:1.)

These expressions are characteristic of Biblical worship. Words such as "Praise the Lord," "O sing to the Lord," "Rejoice in the Lord," "Bless the Lord," open countless Psalms, and run like golden threads through all the worship of the Bible. Praise and adoration are again man's response to God. God is Creator, Redeemer, and Lord. Because of this, man is to bow before Him in adoration and thanksgiving, acknowledging that life and all good gifts come from His hand. To acknowledge this is to glorify God, it is to magnify His supreme worth.

Such acknowledgment, however, must be made not only by lips but by life. True adoration of God issues in obedience to the will of God. Praise expresses itself in life's common tasks. Work may become worship. Worship should issue in work. We are assured that "they who wait for the Lord shall renew their strength." (Isaiah 40:31.) The strength is given that we may be able to carry out God's will in life, and stand up to the tasks to which He calls us in a world over which He is Lord. Worship, then, is man's response of faith to the creating, redeeming, sustaining, ruling God, expressing itself in glad adoration and obedient action.

It follows from this that the focus of worship is the glory of God, not the good of man. In modern worship services too much attention is directed toward what happens to the worshiper. Devices of sound, lighting, symbolism, liturgy, and pageantry are frequently utilized to produce emotional feelings in the worshiper. Those who participate tend to evaluate the worship service in terms of how it "lifted them up" or gave them "a good feeling" or "inspired" them. This is to substitute what someone has called "subjective affection" for "objective trust." It is quite possible to mistake the aesthetic enjoyment which comes from a choral rendition by the choir, or the architectural beauty of a church building, for a true worship experience. Religious entertainment is often confused with religious worship.

Furthermore, to evaluate worship by what happens in the experience of the worshiper is to make men, not God, the center of worship. Worship then becomes a device to use God for human ends, a tool for manipulating divine power and making God a slave to man. The value of prayer is not what happens to the one who prays. The value of prayer is that he has prayed. If he has prayed sincerely, he has thus acknowledged God to be God, and himself to be but a creature who belongs to God and who lives under His Lordship. If uplift comes to the one who has prayed, well and good. The end of prayer, however, is not human delight, but the glory of God. It is not God's chief end to glorify man and to make him enjoy himself forever. It is rather man's chief end to glorify God, and to enjoy Him forever. And this is the end of all true worship.

The Necessity for Corporate Worship

The corporateness of the church discussed earlier in this book has its application to worship. Worship is not a solo, it is a chorus. It is the family of God gathering in His presence to glorify Him. It is each believer coming together with other believers to realize their oneness as the people of God. "Let us consider how to stir up one another to love and good works, not neglecting to meet together, as is the habit of some, but encouraging one another," is the exhortation of an apostolic writer. (Hebrews 10:24-25.) J. B. Phillips puts this in modern parlance by translating it, "Let us not hold aloof from our church meetings, as some do."

This was not merely the opinion of one New Testament writer, nor the advice of an ambitious minister who wanted to have a good attendance record to include in his annual report. It was rather an expression of the essentially corporate nature of the church. As we saw earlier, to be in Christ is to be in the church, which is Christ's body. Although one's relation to Christ involves personal decision, yet to be saved means to be saved "in community rather than in solitariness." To be saved means that we "belong" to the company of the saved. Calvin saw this so clearly that he wrote: "Apart from the Body of Christ, and the fellowship of the godly, there can be no hope of reconciliation with God." At this point Protestantism agrees with Romanism in holding that "outside the church there is no salvation." The difference between Protestant and Romanist on this point is in their definition of the church. The Romanist means there is no salvation outside the Roman Catholic Church, the institutional organization with pope and bishops as its authenticating mark. The Protestant means by the church the fellowship of believers, whose mark is the gift of the Holy Spirit.

The Holy Spirit was given not to isolated individuals, but to the church. To have the gift of the Holy Spirit, therefore, places one automatically in the fellowship of the body to whom the Holy Spirit is given. And outside this body there is no salvation. To fail to worship with God's people regularly and to share in the total life of the people of God, yet to claim to be a Christian, is a flat contradiction in terms. If exceptions to this rule are pointed out, they only confirm the fact that the exceptive cases do not understand their own faith. "All who believed were together" is the earliest description of the church. (Acts 2:44.) It is an abiding mark of the church's life in all generations.

The Place of Ritual in Worship

Ritual is defined as "the form or forms of conducting worship." It is the means by which the people of God order their united approach to God in worship. Some ritual is necessary in any corporate worship. The amount and type of ritual used varies with the various denominations. The Quakers seek to eliminate as much ritual as possible, whereas the so-called "catholic" groups use very elaborate ritual. In any case, some ritual is necessary wherever group worship is held. Even to meet in one place and to await the leading of the Holy Spirit as to who should speak, as the Quakers do, is so far a simple ritual. Ritual has been called by someone "God's table manners." It is fitting that we should approach God in an orderly, mannerly, dignified way to acknowledge Him as King of kings and Lord of lords. Ritual, therefore, in itself is both necessary and good.

Three cautions, however, must be raised in connection with ritual. First, though table manners are good, in a family they must not be allowed to inhibit all spontaneity. In the intimacies of the home rudeness never has any place, but there is always place for the spontaneous expression of love and the informal interchange of heart with heart. Too much rigid formality would turn a family into a gathering of stilted acquaintances. Too careful attention to decorum could be the means of estrangement rather than the bond of love.

In his essay on manners, Emerson insists that the best manners grow out of absolute sincerity. He argued that one could get down on the floor and play with a child in the drawing room and still be well-mannered if he were sincere in this act. To be well-mannered at God's table, therefore, does not always mean to follow stated forms with exactness. It means rather the free, spontaneous, sincere expression of love, the glad outflow of communion with God in whatever forms are best suited to the occasion.

Since corporate worship includes a group, individuals in the group must control their individuality in such a way as not to offend the sensibilities of others. Confusion and chaos do not glorify God. The "manifestation of the Spirit," said Paul, is given "for the common good." (1 Corinthians 12:7.) In a body, foot, hand, ear, and eye must be co-ordinated so that they may function as a unity. Therefore, Paul counseled, "Let all things be done for edification. . . . so that *all* may learn and *all* be encouraged . . . For God is not a God of confusion but of peace." (1 Corinthians 14:26, 31, 33.) Within the limits of decorum and dignity worthy of the presence of God, however, we should be free to set aside or transform our stated ritual under the leadership of the Holy Spirit at any time. Table manners, yes. But not the rigid type which impede rather than regulate the intimate fellowship of the family of God.

A second caution about ritual is this: good manners which are merely externally kept, but do not express the true feelings of the heart, become an unbearable hypocrisy. They degrade rather than exalt human relationships. Likewise, religious ritual which is performed with external correctness merely to be formally polite to God or to maintain a long-standing tradition, becomes an unforgivable hypocrisy which God hates. Isaiah voiced God's judgment on those who "honor me with their lips, while their hearts are far from me." (Isaiah 29:13.) Jesus declared that God preferred the open rebellion of the publicans and harlots to the polite and effuse religious exercises of the Pharisees. (Matthew 21:31.)

Throughout the generations ritual has often been substituted for heart religion. The prophets again and again inveighed against ritual which had no religious reality behind it. "What to me is the multitude of your sacrifices?" cried God through Isaiah. "I have had enough of burnt offerings of rams and the fat of fed beasts." (Isaiah 1:11.) Offerings were "vain," the burning of incense was an "abomination." Why? Because ritual had become a formal cloak for sin. The more disloyal to God the people became in their hearts, the more religious they became in the form of elaborate ritual. Micah spoke in the same vein when he said,

> "With what shall I come before the Lord,
>   and bow myself before God on high?
> Shall I come before him with burnt offerings,
>   with calves a year old?

Will the Lord be pleased with thousands of rams,
    with ten thousands of rivers of oil?" (Micah 6:6-7.)

He answers his questions thus:

"He has showed you, O man, what is good;
    and what does the Lord require of you
but to do justice, and to love kindness,
    and to walk humbly with your God?" (Micah 6:8.)

The psalmist echoes this truth when he writes:

"For thou hast no delight in sacrifice;
    were I to give a burnt offering, thou wouldst not be pleased.
The sacrifice acceptable to God is a broken spirit;
    a broken and contrite heart, O God, thou wilt not despise."
    (Psalm 51:16-17.)

Jesus took up this refrain when He said to men who were meticulous about ritual observance, "Go and learn what this means, 'I desire mercy, and not sacrifice.' " (Matthew 9:13.) The prophets and Jesus were not ruling ritual out of the life of God's people. They were saying rather that when ritual ceases to express the heart relationship of the worshiper to God, it becomes an impediment rather than an aid, a shield behind which to hide the soul's true condition rather than the means of approach to God. The meaning of ritual must be continually re-examined, so that it becomes the channel of true devotion rather than a substitute for it.

A third caution concerning ritual is that it be utilized as a means of receiving God's grace and responding to it rather than something done by man or in the name of man. In the book of Exodus, worship follows redemption and law. First, God acted in behalf of man when he was helpless to do anything for himself. This is grace—God's free and undeserved action for man's deliverance. Then comes the giving of the Law. This was the form man's gratitude was to take—obedience to God in life. Finally, worship was instituted. It was designed to remind the people of God's redemption, to depict the fact that He was now, as of old, their present Redeemer, and to give means of expressing their gratitude for it. It was also to prompt their obedience to God's will in life. This is the purpose of ritual, however much or little of it is used in worship. It is designed as an orderly means of reminding us of God's redeeming mercy and of the demand for obedient response to His will which His grace lays upon us. When ritual becomes a human performance, an end in itself, with its center on man rather than on God, it must be rescued from the ritualists and transformed into an instrument for God's glory.

The Elements of Worship

In the worship of the Reformed Church, the Word of God is central. Whatever confronts the worshiper with that Word is acceptable. Whatever does not is objectionable. But what is the Word of God? In the Bible, the Word of God is always something more than mere words in print or mere sounds which fall on ears. God's Word is His act, *the giving of Himself* to men. The supreme place where He has given Himself to men is in the gift of Jesus Christ. Supremely, therefore, Jesus is God's Word. The criterion by which worship is to be measured is the degree to which it confronts men with God's act in Christ, and leads them either to salvation or to judgment. God's Word is Christ acting in behalf of men in such fashion that He produces a reaction in men, either of acceptance or rejection.

But how are men confronted by Christ? There are two primary means—the reading of the Bible and the preaching and teaching of it. Historically, preaching and teaching preceded the Bible. In our times, the Bible becomes the prior authority for all true preaching and teaching. The reason for this is that the Bible is the permanent record of what the early church preached and taught about Jesus. It thereby is the source of our knowledge of Jesus and the norm by which our understanding of Him is to be determined. The final authority for faith and the only authoritative source for preaching and teaching is the Bible.

The authority which the Bible carries, however, is not an external authority. It is rather an intrinsic authority, a self-authenticating authority to faith, because through it God actually speaks to us now. The books in the Bible did not become authoritative because the church put them in the Bible. On the other hand, the church put them in the Bible because they already had assumed an authority over the church. The church did not give them their authority, it merely recognized the authority which was intrinsically theirs. The Holy Spirit used these books to confront men with God's redeeming love in Christ. And so the church accepted them on the basis of their intrinsic authority witnessed to by the Holy Spirit. For this reason, the Bible is central in Reformed worship. It is to be read, preached, and taught. Even congregational singing is to bear witness to its message, and the prayers should breathe its atmosphere. The whole service of worship should make real and contemporary the redeeming action of God in Jesus Christ to which the Bible bears witness.

The most vital way in which the redeeming action of God in Christ is made known to man is through preaching. In true preaching Christ, the living Word of God, makes Himself known through the Scriptures as they are interpreted by the preacher. When one has come to believe through the Bible what God has done in Christ, and then declares it to others, God Himself speaks through that declaration and offers men His salvation. "So faith comes from what is heard," wrote Paul, "and what is heard comes by the preaching of Christ." (Romans 10:17.) The sermon, therefore, rather than being an adjunct to the worship service, or a dull speech which must be tolerated by the congregation, should be the very heart and climax of worship.

In dealing with the relation of God to man, the Bible habitually uses the terms of hearing rather than seeing. We do not find God through the open vision of the mystic. God makes Himself known by speaking. The most effective way God has of speaking is through the proclamation of His Word by preachers. This is true, of course, only when preachers preach Christ as He is presented in the Bible. And even then, it is only as the Holy Spirit takes the word of the preacher and makes it God's Word that men hear God speak through preaching. But when the Bible is preached, and the Holy Spirit is given free course through the preacher's word, preaching becomes the most effective way by which God communicates Himself to men.

True preaching is not merely an action of man, it is an action of God. It is God's mercy in Christ made living in this hour. Preaching, therefore, has always been central in the worship of the Reformed churches, who conceive worship to be concerned with God and what He is doing. In preaching, God initiates His redeeming action to which man is to respond in gratitude and obedience. Teaching is another form of declaring the gospel, differing in method but not in content. Hence, preaching and teaching are two forms of the same activity. It is only as the gospel is declared and taught that the Reformed faith can survive in the world.

In addition to the reading of the Scriptures, and preaching and teaching based on them, there are other elements of worship. The singing of hymns and psalms is a means of man's responding to God's grace in praise and adoration. For this reason, the value of singing, whether choral or congregational, does not lie in the quality of the music nor in its aesthetic contribution to the participants. It lies in the sincerity and intelligence with which it is used as a channel of true praise. Singing without clarity of words, therefore, or with words which are sentimental or man-centered rather than reflective of the glory of God, is to be rejected in Protestant worship services.

Prayer, too, is a definite part of worship. In prayer the congregation unitedly bows before God to own Him as Creator, Redeemer, Sustainer, and Lord. It is man's way of recognizing that all his fountains are in God, that apart from Him man can do nothing. It is also a means of offering ourselves to God as instruments of His will, as obedient servants whose purpose in life it is to strive for those things which God wants done in the world.

Most worship services include an offering also. This is as it should be. The offering is not an intrusion of mundane or secular matters into worship. It is rather an opportunity for the worshipers to give concrete expression to their obedient response to God's grace. Do we love God because of His grace? Do we desire His will to be done on earth as it is in heaven? Are we willing to be the instruments of that will even when it costs? These issues are answered less by what we say than by what is indicated when the offering is taken. The use a man makes of his money is a good test of his devotion and a measure of his obedience. The offering also symbolizes the dedication of the whole of life—the toil by which we earn our money, the things for which it is spent, and the use of our time, talents, and influence.

The Sacraments

Two other elements of worship should be given special attention. They are the sacraments of Baptism and the Lord's Supper. The sacraments have posed many problems for the church throughout the years. It is difficult even to define them. But in simplest terms, they have been described as the *verbum visibile,* the Word of God made visible. They are outward signs which confirm the inward action of the Holy Spirit in the heart of the believer. Since they are visible signs of the Word of God, they have no meaning apart from the Word. It is only as they confirm the preaching of the Word that they are of value. If separated from it, they become magic. Since they are a part of the church's worship and belong to the preaching of the Word, they are functions of the congregation, and should normally take place only in the gathered assembly of the people of God rather than in private meetings.

Baptism is the act which confirms one's being brought into the household of faith, one's birth into the family of God. It suggests that the one baptized has died with Christ, been buried with Him, and has risen to new life. (Romans 6:4.) It is much more, then, than a mere symbol or sentiment. It is the confirmation of God's gift of Himself to the believer. In the sacrament *God acts, God gives Himself.* A baptism, therefore, is not a "christening" or a "dedication," both of which are acts of man. It is rather a sign of God's gift of Himself by which one is justified in believing that he is God's child and a member of His family.

Arguments concerning the correct mode of baptism are quite beside the point. It is the meaning of baptism rather than its mode which is important. The main point of discussion is whether it is proper to baptize infants. To this the Reformed Churches have always given an affirmative answer. Those who oppose this fail in their understanding of the corporate nature of the church. To insist that one can be baptized only on his own faith is to hold that the body of Christ is made up of an aggregate of individual believers, which is no body at all but a loose collection of members. A child of Christian parents, baptized into the church by God's action in the congregation of His people, may be given God's grace through the faith of the church, whether he is aware of it or not. God's action in our behalf is not limited to our faith nor to our consciousness of what is happening.

To hold otherwise would be like saying that when a baby is born nothing has happened because the baby does not know it, or that nothing takes place when a mother feeds her child because the child does not know that she is his mother nor that he is being fed. A child of Christian parents, by virtue of being "in" his parents who are in the church, is already in the church of Christ. Baptism does not make him a member of the church. It confirms that fact. When the child comes to the years of discretion, he must make his own choice whether he will accept his membership in Christ's body or cut himself off from it. But he does not decide whether to enter God's people. *He decides whether to stay in or get out!*

If baptism signifies that a child is a member of the congregation of God's people, then it should be done in the worship of the congregation. God acts in the sacrament, and the whole congregation must respond to His action for the child. Private parties, cheap sentiment, and attention to the cuteness of the behavior of the baby are quite beside the point, and should be eliminated.

The Lord's Supper has a threefold significance. For one thing, it is a remembrance of God's saving act in Christ. It carries us back to the upper room where Jesus' last supper was held with His disciples. There He broke bread and gave it to them, saying, "Take; this is my body." Also He took a cup and gave to them to drink, saying, "This is my blood of the covenant, which is poured out for many." (Mark 14:22-24.) And, according to Paul, He commanded, "Do this in remembrance of me." (1 Corinthians 11:24.) The Lord's Supper, then, in visible form recalls Jesus' saving death in our behalf.

The Lord's Supper, however, is not only a memorial. It is also a present communion or participation with Christ. "The cup of blessing which we bless," said Paul, "is it not a participation in the blood of Christ? The bread which we break, is it not a participation in the body of Christ?" (1 Corinthians 10:16.) In the Lord's Supper, the Christ who gave Himself to men on a cross is present, giving Himself to them anew. As the visible elements of bread and wine are taken in and become a part of us, so Christ is given to us by faith. His life becomes our life. In the Communion service Paul's experience becomes ours: "I have been crucified with Christ; it is no longer I who live, but Christ who lives in me." (Galatians 2:20.)

A third aspect of the Lord's Supper is that it is a proclamation of a hope. Through this service we "proclaim the Lord's death until he comes." (1 Corinthians 11:26.) We witness to the fact that a day is coming when the whole family of God shall sit down at His table and be fed by Christ in the Kingdom yet to come. The Lord's Supper kindles this hope, and witnesses ever afresh to its reality.

Thus baptism is the visible sign of our entrance into God's family, and the Lord's Supper is the continual renewal of all that God has done for us, is doing, and will yet do at the end of the age. The sacraments are more than mere symbols. Something happens in them. God acts through them. But the action is dependent not on the visible symbols, but on the faith which accompanies them, the church's response to God's action. The visible signs themselves, therefore, must never be allowed to assume too great an importance. Otherwise they may become idols obscuring the realities which lie beneath them. Nor should they ever be separated from the preaching and teaching of the Word. God's Word always takes priority, and the spoken Word must always attend the Word made visible in the sacraments.

If in the sacraments God actually gives Himself to men, is there no giving of Himself apart from the sacraments? For example, if a child should die unbaptized, is he outside God's favor? Surely not. The sacrament merely confirms God's gift of Himself prior to its action. If this is so, then why have sacraments? An illustration may serve to answer this.

A wedding ceremony does not make a marriage. It merely confirms the self-giving of the couple to each other in their decision to get married. And yet, although in their decision to marry the couple have pledged themselves to each other, still in the vows taken at the wedding there is a renewal and a confirmation of the self-giving which is more than mere symbol—it is *an act through which the self-giving is sealed.* Presumably, if a couple gave themselves with absolute fidelity to each other and lived in faithfulness through the years, they would be married in the sight of God even though no wedding ceremony were performed. And yet we would hardly say that for this reason weddings are unnecessary. *Normally,* at least, the wedding is necessary to confirm what is already a fact, and so to renew that fact that it becomes a more meaningful fact.

Thus it is with the sacraments. One might be loved of God and love Him in return without Baptism and the Lord's Supper. But normally, the confirmation and deepening of the mutual love is done through the sacraments, which ought never to be neglected in the life of the church.

10

The Unity of the Church

When one travels abroad, he is often asked what his nationality is. Unless he is hopelessly provincial, he would not answer, "I am a Missourian," or "I am a North Dakotan." He would reply, "I am an American." His identity as a member of the whole nation is more important than his specific location within the nation, or the peculiar characteristics of the locality where he lives.

It is equally strange when one is asked what his religious faith is for him to answer, "I am a Presbyterian," or "I am a Methodist." The correct answer would be, "I am a Christian." One often hears someone describing another by saying, "He is of the Baptist faith," or "He was reared in the Lutheran faith." Such statements are basically incorrect. There is no Baptist faith, or Lutheran faith, or Presbyterian faith, or Episcopal faith. There is only the *Christian* faith. True faith in Christ is exactly the same thing whether the one who has it be a Quaker, a Congregationalist, a Presbyterian, or an Anglo-Catholic. One's relation to Christ is quite above the particular denomination to which he belongs.

The Church by Nature One

This suggests that the unity of the church is a fact of supreme importance, far more significant than the fact that there are many denominations within the one church. This is true because by nature the church is one. Jesus did not come to found *churches*. He came to found a *church*. He did not say, when Peter confessed His Messiahship, "On this rock I will build my churches," but "On this rock I will build my church, and the powers of death shall not prevail against it [not "them"]." (Matthew 16:18.)

When the church which Jesus founded first took shape, it was one church, not many. We have already seen in chapter 2 how one of its marked characteristics was its unity. Futhermore, the unity of the church is confirmed by the teaching of the New Testament. The Fourth Gospel interprets the death of Jesus as the means of gathering "into one the children of God who are scattered abroad." (John 11:52.) This means two things: first, that men who are alienated from God by sin become children of God once more through Jesus' death; and second, that when they become children of God they are *one* with all of God's children. This oneness of those who are in Christ, moreover, is as absolute as the oneness between Jesus and His Father. This is clearly pointed out from Jesus' high priestly prayer, wherein He prayed for His people, "that they may be one, even as we are one." (John 17:11.) Christians within the church are as indissolubly one as is Jesus with the Father.

Paul reinforced this when he counselled the Ephesians to "maintain the unity of the Spirit in the bond of peace." (Ephesians 4:3.) The reasoning by which he undergirded this was that the nature of the church demands it. "There is one body and one Spirit," he wrote, "just as you were called to the one hope that belongs to your call, one Lord, one faith, one baptism, one God and Father of us all, who is above all and through all and in all." (Ephesians 4:4-6.) Examine the elements of this statement: The church is one body, and that body lives by the one Holy Spirit animating it. Christians, therefore, are united as the various members of a body belong to each other, and all share the very same spiritual life. Furthermore, the hope of salvation is the same for all Christians. We are all saved by the same Lord, we have all appropriated His salvation by the same faith, which we have all witnessed by the same act of entrance into the church—baptism. This multiplied oneness is real because of the fact that every element of it is related to the "God and Father of us all," who is one—the One who reigns over us all, who works through us all, and who lives in us all.

Not only did Paul teach this, but he witnessed to it by costly action. The latter years of his life were dominated by a passion to maintain the unity of the church. Differences of theological judgment had arisen over the inclusion of the Gentiles in the church. Many of the Jews argued that since Christianity sprang from Judaism, it was necessary for a Gentile to be circumcised and to keep the Jewish Law in order to be a Christian. Paul countered this with all his might. He insisted that Christ had died for all men, Jew and Gentile alike, and that He now offered salvation to all to be appropriated solely by faith and not by keeping the Law. Hence, he argued, Gentiles may believe in Jesus and become full-fledged members of the church without first being circumcised and coming through the door of Judaism.

Although Paul maintained this view with unflinching zeal and refused to yield an inch on it, yet he could not bear to see the church split over this issue. Differences there were, but the differences must be held within the one church. While he would not allow the Judaizers to foist the Jewish Law upon the Gentiles, he did not try to exclude from the church the Jews who kept the Law. They were at liberty to keep the Law if they wanted to, and he, as a Jew, made personal concessions to them by himself observing for their sakes certain stipulations of the Law which really meant nothing to him. (See Acts 21:20-26.) But with all his might he contended that these Christian Jews who kept the Law and the Christian Gentiles who did not were in the same church.

In order to dramatize this unity, Paul gathered up an offering throughout his Gentile churches to take up to the mother church at Jerusalem, as a token of the fact that in spite of their differences of outlook and observance, they were still one in Christ. (See 1 Corinthians 16:1-4; 2 Corinthians 9:1-5.) He was so eager to make this gesture of oneness that he finally risked his life to do it. As he journeyed up toward Jerusalem with the offering he had gathered, he was aware that trouble awaited him there. (Acts 20:22-23.) His friends tried to dissuade him from his purpose, and "begged him not to go up to Jerusalem." (Acts 21: 12.) But he insisted on going at any cost. He told the elders of Ephesus of whom he was taking farewell, "I do not account my life of any value . . . if only I may accomplish my course and the ministry which I received from the Lord Jesus, to testify to the gospel of the grace of God." (Acts 20:24.) He said to his friends in Caesarea, "I am ready not only to be imprisoned but even to die at Jerusalem for the name of the Lord Jesus." (Acts 21:13.)

Why was Paul so determined to go to Jerusalem at the risk of his life? It was because of his passion to maintain the unity of the church. If, by taking the gifts of his Gentile Christians to the Jewish Christians at Jerusalem, he could dramatize the fact that they were all one in Christ, and members one of another, that would be well worth the giving of his life. For a part of the "gospel of the grace of God" which had been delivered to him to preach was the unity of the church. To maintain this unity he was ready to die.

Disunity the Result of Sin

If the church is by nature one, what has happened to it in our modern world? One of the outstanding marks of the church today is its disunity and brokenness. There are between 250 and 300 separate church bodies in the United States. And the number is continually increasing. "The scandal of our divisions" is a phrase which is often used to describe the modern church. And many there are outside the church who question the value of the church's word to a divided and broken world because the church cannot heal its own division.

When we look at the actual condition of the church in the light of the New Testament presentation of its unity, we can only conclude that the present disunity is the result of sin. Somewhere along the line the church has failed to understand her own nature. And this failure cannot be accounted for merely by a lack of understanding. It is an ugly fact which can be explained only by the frank admission that the disunity wrought in the world by sin has been allowed to creep into the church and to leave its mark there. When the church divides at any place, it is the result of sin, either on the part of those who leave it or those who thrust them out, or both. And it is well to recall here what was mentioned earlier in this book, that vital reformers of the church's life have seldom divided the church by their choice. They have rather desired to reform the church's life from within, and have separated only when forced out by those who refused to reform.

This means that we should not glory in our divisions, but repent of them, and work for their healing. To accept our present divisions as right, or to seek to perpetuate them, or even to go so far as deliberately to foster new divisions, is to try to destroy the Body of Christ, and is thus a thrust at Christ Himself. Christ cannot be divided, nor can His Body, the church, remain divided save at the cost of weakness and failure. And those who, in the name of "separation," are advocating new rends in the Body of Christ, are, whether they know it or not, seeking to assassinate Christ. If they do not know this, then they can only be prayed for, "Father, forgive them; for they know not what they do." The purity of the church of Christ is to be secured by clearing up the blood stream, not by severing its members one from another. No person or movement, therefore, which seeks to rend Christ's members one from another should be followed or encouraged, no matter whatever else their spiritual excellencies may be. A deliberately schismatic person, the central drive of whose work it is to separate Christians one from another, is either deluded or bad. In either case, he is not to be followed.

Excuses for Disunity

It is easy to hide from the problem of disunity by rationalization. We have become so accustomed to the divisions in the Body of Christ that it is natural to accept them as right. Familiarity and custom brand them as normal. The various denominations, therefore, are tempted to be content with pursuing their own program, as though they had little or no concern with the life of the whole church, of which they are a very small part. This leads to the assumption that one member of a body may fulfill its function in detachment from the other members of the body.

Paul answered this strange doctrine when he wrote, "For the body does not consist of one member but of many. If the foot should say, 'Because I am not a hand, I do not belong to the body,' that would not make it any less a part of the body. And if the ear should say, 'Because I am not an eye, I do not belong to the body,' that would not make it any less a part of the body." (1 Corinthians 12:14-16.) Therefore, he concluded, "The eye cannot say to the hand, 'I have no need of you,' nor again the head to the feet, 'I have no need of you.'" (1 Corinthians 12:21.) No, if the various denominations are members of a body, they cannot adequately function in isolation from the other members of that body. A body is whole only as all its members are co-ordinated into a unity, and each member fulfills its proper function only as it relates itself to the activity of all the other members.

What are some of the excuses by which we avoid the logic of this? Some avoid it by the easy affirmation that they are the whole church, and that all other denominations are outside the Body of Christ. This has traditionally been the view of the Roman Church. The Eastern Orthodox Church tends in this direction, too, as well as some of the newer and smaller sects who claim absoluteness for themselves. The logic of this, however, is that one of the members of the body is the whole body. To this Paul replied, "For the body does not consist of one member but of many. . . . If all were a single organ, where would the body be?" (1 Corinthians 12:14, 19.) As we have seen earlier, the church is made up of all those to whom Christ has given Himself by His Holy Spirit. To cut many of these off, and to say that only what is left is the Body of Christ, is to dismember the Body and to end with a mutilated torso.

Another excuse given is that the unity of the church is a spiritual unity, which remains in spite of the external disunity. For this reason, it is said, we need not concern ourselves about the outward divisions in the church, but can rest assured that the church is one in the realm of the unseen. Two things make this view questionable. First, granted that the unity of a body consists in the one life which animates it rather than in its visible organization, can this one life vitalize all the members of a body if they are detached from each other? Second, the Bible is crassly physical in dealing with spiritual realities. It does not believe in disembodied spirits. A "spiritualism" which can believe in the sort of spiritual unity which is not seeking to embody itself in visible ways is wholly foreign to the Scriptures. If the church is one spiritually, then its lack of unity in the concrete, visible realities of its life is a denial of its nature, and cries out for remedy.

A third excuse for our divisions is that known as the "branch theory" of the church. According to this view, the various denominations are different branches of the same tree. The reason for these different branches lies in the differences of temperament among people, and the differences of social or historical conditioning, which naturally tend to make those of like mind unite and form distinct groups within the church. In so far as this view sees that there should be diversity within the church, it is creditable. But to utilize this to justify the division of the church into the exclusive denominations we now know, as though this were the highest will of God, is to allow sociology to take over theology. Sociological factors which create differences would never have been allowed, in the days of the New Testament, to offset the theology that the church is one. Whatever differences there may be within people and movements, these should enrich the life of the whole church rather than being the justification of fragmentizing the church.

No, if the church is one, as the New Testament insists, our excuses for failing to realize this oneness will not hold up. We shall be in a much better position to face them realistically if we admit that they are not willed by God, but are rather the result of our sin. This will replace complacency with concern, and pride with penitence.

Unity, Not Uniformity

The unity of the church, however, is not to be confused with uniformity. Diversity there is, and should be, within the church. But diversity may exist without disunity. There is diversity within a large family—different aptitudes, different tastes, different personal characteristics. It would be a strange family, nonetheless, which would set up separate living arrangements to satisfy the particular peculiarities of each member. In a real family, the diversity is held within the unity of the family. The family lives in the same house, eats together, carries forward its group activities as a unity. In this way, the diversity of tastes enriches the whole family life, and each benefits from the other.

Likewise, within the church there is a rich diversity. Uniformity is neither desirable nor possible. "Men have different gifts," said Paul, "but it is the same Spirit Who gives them. There are different ways of serving God, but it is the same Lord Who is served. God works through different men in different ways, but it is the same God Who achieves His purposes through them all." (1 Corinthians 12:4-6, Phillips' translation.) But the point to which Paul was driving in speaking of the varieties of gifts within the church was this: "To each is given the manifestation of the Spirit for the common good." (1 Corinthians 12:7.) These various manifestations of the Spirit were not to be used as the basis for developing different branches within the church. They were rather to enrich the total life of the one church. They were various functions of the members of one body.

There will always be, and there should be, rich diversity within God's family. Uniformity of doctrine, ritual, or church structure is not of the essence of the church. If such uniformity should prevail, it would immeasurably impoverish the church's life. Unity is an organic thing, vital enough to unite differences and to make them serve each other, and together serve the whole. Many stones, but one temple. Many members, but one body.

Unity a Gift of God

It is always to be remembered, however, in our striving after unity, that it is a gift of God, not a human achievement. We cannot, by human decision and organizational effort, make the church one. The church is already one, made so by the creative act of God. It is ours merely to *realize* the unity which we already have in Christ, and to *manifest* it by word and deed to the world. As an individual Christian has to become what he is, so the church must become what it is. It is already one, but it must become one. This may sound like a paradox, but it is a New Testament paradox.

When Paul was dealing with the problem of threatened disunity in the Philippian church, he wrote, "Have this mind among yourselves, *which you have in Christ Jesus.*" (Philippians 2:5.) Their unity was not something for them to achieve. They already had it in Christ. It was theirs only to realize what was already God's gift to them. Likewise, when writing to the Ephesian church about maintaining "the unity of the Spirit in the bond of peace" (Ephesians 4:3), Paul indicated that they were to maintain that which was already theirs in the nature of the case. "There is one body and one Spirit," he wrote. (Ephesians 4:4.) They were not to make the body one. They were to realize that it was one. But how was this realization to come? They were to grow into it by love—"we are to grow up in every way into him who is the head, into Christ, from whom the whole body, joined and knit together by every joint with which it is supplied, when each part is working properly, makes bodily growth and upbuilds itself in love." (Ephesians 4:15-16.) Just as our salvation is given to us now only as a foretaste, while its fullness is reserved for the final coming of the Kingdom, so the unity of the church is given to us as a foretaste but will be fully realized in the age to come. It is the drag of our sin which keeps us from realizing it fully now. For this reason, our disunity should be a constant cause of penitence. And as we grow in grace, we should likewise grow in the realization of the unity which is ours in Christ.

Unity and the Ecumenical Movement

The ecumenical movement is the thing which marks our generation off from all earlier generations of Protestants as unique. It is what the late Archbishop Temple called "the great new fact of our era." It is significant that when the secular world is breaking apart and deepening the rifts which divide men, the church has begun to take more seriously than at any time since the Reformation the meaning of her own unity. The word "ecumenical" is not a good one, but has to be used for want of a better. It means literally "world-wide" or "that which includes the inhabited world." It is quite akin to the word "catholic" or "universal," but because that word has been taken over so largely by one part of the church, the word "ecumenical" is perhaps the better one to express the church's unity in our time.

The ecumenical movement, which has eventuated in the World Council of Churches, is a united effort by many members of the Body of Christ to move toward a realization of the church's true unity. It is not an effort, as some allege, to make one world church organization, a super-church, which shall wield authority from above over all Christians. The majority of those who are most active in the World Council of Churches are most aware of the deep differences which divide Christians in our time, and of the long and difficult road ahead in trying even to approximate the actual unity of the church. They are determined, however, in spite of differences of doctrine, liturgy, and organization "to stay together." The differences which divide the churches are less important than the fact that they are one in Christ. The World Council is an effort, through penitence and faith, to witness to the world the church's unity in Christ, and to follow, if even afar off, the One whose prayer for His church was that it should be one. (See John 17.) It is the one significant symbol in our time that the church desires really to be the church, by growing up "in every way into him who is the head, into Christ" (Ephesians 4:15), and thus upbuild itself in love.

I have tried in this work to avoid lengthy quotations from modern writers. I cannot, however, refrain from bringing it to a close by some words from the late Archbishop Temple, who before his untimely death was one of the most significant figures in the ecumenical movement and one of the founders of the World Council of Churches:

"The unity which the Lord prays His disciples may enjoy is that which is eternally characteristic of the Triune God. It is therefore something more than a means to any end . . . it is itself the one worthy end of all human aspiration; it is the life of heaven . . . Before the loftiness of that hope and calling our little experience of unity and fellowship is humbled to the dust. Our friendships, our reconciliations, our unity of spirit in Church gatherings or in missionary conferences—beautiful as they are, and sometimes even wonderful in comparison with our habitual life of sectional rivalries and tensions, yet how poor and petty they appear in the light of the Lord's longing. Let all of us who are concerned in. . . 'Conversations' with fellow-Christians of other denominations, take note of the judgment under which we stand by virtue of the gulf separating the level of our highest attainment and noblest enterprise, from 'the prize of the call upwards which God gives in Christ Jesus'—*that they may be one as we.*"*

* Quoted from F. A. Iremonger, *William Temple*, pp. 389-390, by permission of Oxford University Press.

THE NATURE AND MISSION OF THE CHURCH pictures the church as God's answer to the tragedy of broken relationships between man and God. In showing how this answer is communicated to the world, Dr. Miller focuses on the church's nature, life, history, Lord, faith, mission, form, purity, worship, and unity.

". . . profitable to anyone who is trying to understand more fully the nature of the church and the problems which Christians face in the matter of reunion."—**Interpretation**

DONALD G. MILLER is president of Pittsburgh Theological Seminary. Before coming to Pittsburgh in 1962, he was Professor of New Testament at Union Theological Seminary in Virginia for twenty years. Dr. Miller has written the volume on Luke in the **Layman's Bible Commentary.**